SAILORS OF SCIENCE

Introduction to 21 Scientists' Life, Work and their Dreams

SAILORS OF SCIENCE

Introduction to 21 Scientists' Life, Work and their Dreams

By

Dr. Vishwanath Shankarrao Patil

DPH

DISCOVERY PUBLISHING HOUSE PVT. LTD.

NEW DELHI-110 002

Published by:
Tilak Wasan
DISCOVERY PUBLISHING HOUSE PVT. LTD.
4831/24, Ansari Road, Prahlad Street
Darya Ganj, New Delhi-110002 (India)
Phone: +91-11-23279245, 43764432
Fax: +91-11-23253475
E-mail: parul.wasan@gmail.com
info@discoverypublishinggroup.com
web: www.discoverypublishinggroup.com

***First Edition:* 2011**
ISBN: 978-81-8356-729-9

Sailors of Science: ***Introduction to 21 Scientists' Life, Work and their Dreams***

Printed at:
Shree Balaji Art Press
Delhi

To My Hardworking Wife
SHALINI PATIL
and Daughter
NAMRATA PATIL

Contents

Prologue

Right from my school days I had two strong attractions. One was for the teaching profession and the other for reading—especially the biographies and autobiographies of great people. The reason was obvious, my father and my maternal uncle (Shri. Tukaram Hari Pawar) were devoted and renowned primary teachers. They were leaders of the villages where they served. Moreover, the village Paparde (*Tal. Patan, Distt. Satara, Maharashtra* which our family has roots was known for its highest number of primary teachers in my school days. As I was getting educated some- how or the other I could keep in good association with my teachers – young and old, of all subjects and types. This made me still involved in the profession. As a student, I was promising and outstanding. Due to this typical background at home and my association with number of teachers, it was beyond any doubt that I would be a teacher—primary, secondary or college/university. Another major influence on my reading was Patan public library and librarian. When I completed my secondary education, I used to visit library regularly. There was sort of interactive reading between receptive young students and old generation of readers. Young listeners were humble audience for good readings. They used to discuss with us the title lines in the newspapers and what is now realized as "reading between the lines". They would recommend us the books especially biographies and novels of famous writers like Khandekar etc. It then became the habits to read selectively. Reading was continuous and it was very positive for development. In those days Acharya Atre's autobiography was in vogue called '*Karheche Pani*'. My father asked me to read the book called '*Vidhyarthi Seetavam*' revealing the life of Shri. Tawade and many others.

Fortunately, I had good classmates in high school days those were also good readers and later on became important persons in social life. I joined as college teacher (1967) in Shri. Warana Mahavidyalaya. Warananagar, Distt. Kolhapur and there colleagues deeply gave the insight for reading. I remember the visit of Shri. Shivajirao Sawant and long discussions held with him on his miraculous a success of the Novel on Karna's life '*Mrutunjaya*'. During my student days, I was science student so I could hardly get time to devote for reading but as a teacher I could. Later during my Ph. D. stage I was fully involved in scientific pursuit in prestigious National Chemical Laboratory. It kept me starving about general reading but I continued little bit. My joining Sangamner College in 1971 gave me wider exposure to real, varied, responsible and the creative life. College had a spacious and rich library, nice faculty, various innovative programmes in education and importantly conducive educational atmosphere.

I identified myself with the college along with many others. Principal Kaundinya was the leader and S.P. Sanstha Sangamner a high patronage to college activities. It was the place, I dreamt for being a teacher. It gave me the satisfaction of the profession. During the course, I was made vice principal (1974) and some time in 1986 and during 1992-93 I was also made in-charge Principal. I had a long inning as a vice principal and two short innings as in-charge principal. During those days I remained—positively remained as teacher. I desired and is deriving the pleasure of teaching. I tried to contribute in my own little ways. It is not the place to assess but during 1971 to 1993 these 22 years my major time was with college and too with involvement! It gave the experience of the people, by people and for the people. The things accumulated. During discussions with Principal Kaundinya and other colleagues, ideas of writing used to come to mind. We had college activity information broachers like linkage, Shodha Parva (Qwest) and alike. I could be of bit help in their release. I wrote some books about my subjects. They were formal, textual. They gave some joy of creation but not enough.

And things changed! I stayed away from administration and concentrated on teaching. Meanwhile my father expired. I had strong association with him as a friend, philosopher and guide. It made me very miserable. The present book came to me as a solace. I kept on reading about scientists believed in 'The hows and the history of most machinery and people are intimately connected'. I used to tell the students about the evolution of scientific concepts by two ways by scientific method and by meditation. This gives the pleasure of learning and teaching, it inculcates the habit of thinking much needed in education. Now-a-days it has become more bookish and examination oriented. Sometimes during those days, I heard one good lecture in which three points of wisdom were stressed *i.e.*

1. There are some things which are beyond your control; whatever you may do will not have any effect on those things. You should ignore such things.
2. There are some things which could be changed by your efforts to at least some extent. You should concentrate on such things and try your level best and lastly but importantly
3. You should be able to discriminate between the above two things which is of course quite difficult because their line of demarcation is very dismal and unclear. The present book is an attempt to make this line little more clear.

Next came the question of style and way of presentation. There are seven aspects of this

- Informative
- Interesting

- Inspiring
- Interactive
- Innovative
- Informal, and
- Illustrative (7 I's)

Depending on individual scientists personality there 7 aspects were staggered skilfully. Where information was simple, illustration was too small; where information was difficult to digest illustration had an upper hand. For inspiration—scientists were selected who suffered a lot for their findings or rooting their novel ideas in scientific and other community. The list of scientists is sufficient to make my point. Galileo was the first scientist who elaborately used scientific method and explicitly believed in experimentation. The last scientist in the book is Stephen Hawking where thinking/intuition has upper hand to experimentation. During selection of scientists as far as possible in various fields, different types of people was the criteria. Indian scientists selected are :

1. Ramanujan for his very short life, genius and poor health and family background;
2. Jagdish Chandra Bose for his nationalistic outlook and recent report that he was ahead of Marconi in wireless telegraphy; and
3. Chandrashekar because of his patient working for about fifty years through the beginning experience was heart breaking and secondly his meticulous nature.

Herman Mark was selected because my subject was related to Polymer Chemistry. Sumner was selected because of enzymes – wonderful catalysts of nature and he was left handed and lost his left hand in an accident, still he kept on working with right hand. The only female scientist included in the book is Madam Marie Curie. She got two times Nobel Prize. She was the most modest, beautiful, versatile, emotional hardworking nationalist scientists. She suffered a lot in her personal life. She cared for wounded persons during World War I. For them she was an angel of mercy with a beautiful face, tired and acid bitten long fingers. She died a Martyr to her own work.

Edison was technological genius with 1093 patents at his credit. He believed in 'Work is Worship' and 'perspiration'. He was selected as model scientist.

Carver's life is the ideal life that was lived for others especially the poor and innocent lot of Negros. There is no certainty about his birth date because he was born to an insignificant slave Negro parent but his deeds made him great and his passing away is celebrated as Carver's day (5th June). Einstein became the demigod in spite of himself because of his revolutionary ideas. He was far ahead of his times. His work in 1905 was proved in 1919 and that of 1925 in 1995. He was lone star thinker in the scientific world. Mendel was included in the book because he is the father of science of genetics. Linus Pauling is the unique name who got two unshared Nobel Prizes for his outstanding contributions in two altogether different fields.

Pasteur was the prophetic scientist. For him will, work and wait were the three most important words. His business was to heal and not to kill. His achievements were need based and to extend the frontiers of life. Penicillin is referred as the miracle/wonder drug and the name associated with it is Dr. Fleming. He was the brilliant student from the school of life and nature.

Wöhler was selected as he is the father of Organic Chemistry and broke the shekels of vital force theory. Humboldt was the naturalist and could understand the importance of ecological balance long ago. He was self sponsor of his scientific pursuits throughout the life. Computer is the field which was encompassed all our lives. While referring the history and computer development I read many names but not of Professor Kilburn. Accidentally in daily Maharashtra Times, I read one article about Kilburn and his achievements and his modest nature. I collected the material from my son's friend Vishwantaht Kamat of C-Dac Pune and from my son Prashant. Moreover, I wrote to Professor Kilburn directly and he supplied the material about his scientific pursuits, immediately. It was rewarding experience. I tried to refer as much material on various scientists as possible and I wrote to some of the people for authenticity. All experience was really a great pleasure.

As the target of 21 scientists came near and near 'to whom to select and whom to omit' became the problem. Newton and Faraday were must but I have omitted because Galileo, Einstein, Hawking were working in the near by areas of Newton and I had already selected these three. I have no jubilation for omission of Faraday, he should have included. Though scientists selected are twenty one during the write up many other important scientists are referred and unavoidable information about them has naturally came into the text. Prof. Kilburn for example cannot be discussed without name of F.C. Williams. Alexander Fleming will be incomplete without Wright's contribution and so on. Nobel is immortal through his prizes but as a scientist also he was great, so his inclusion was natural.

Feynman was one name which was sponsored by many. He was great as a teacher and researcher. He got the idea of Nobel Prize winning concept in a hotel! It was really the fascinating point about him. His mischievous nature makes me call him as Fun-man but in reality he was fine man too! The day Feynman died; the students at Caltech hung a banner across the 11 storey library building on the campus. The message on the banner read 'WE LOVE YOU DICK'. Around the world, many people who hadn't even met Feynman felt a sense of personal loss when he died. Feynman seems to many like a old friend. He was therefore a must. While preparing the book association with these people enriched my life and I had nice time. I wrote the book because I want to share my joy with all of you – the readers. It is the joy of science, the joy of sacrifice and devotion, the joy of understanding the mysteries of nature and human beings.

The book was written in English but the 1st publisher who came forward to publish the book wanted it to be in Marathi. So I translated it in Marathi. I am grateful to Ranganath Pathare of our college who in the renowned teacher of physics and the most successful creative writer of his age. During book writing immediate audience that I had was my wife Mrs. Shalini Patil and youngest daughter Miss Namrata Patil. So I used to tell them something spontaneously. My wife used to react shapely and noisily. My daughter used to react slowly and patiently. In between my son Prashant, daughter Mamta used to discuss about the scientists. During all these days my family remained active supporter and critic of my work. The second family was that of Kapre. Mrs. Rupali Kapre, her husband Dr Kapre and their daughter Miss Ruta had active role. Mrs. Kapre had major share in translation and criticism. There are so many others whose support must be mentioned my brother A.S. Patil who is scientist in NCL Pune, Fergusson college library staff, my college library staff, many of my friends are amongst them.

Finally I trust that you will enjoy reading the book because of these great people. My role was to just open their work and life before you in my own way and limitations. I have tried to make the work up to date. Your suggestions will be highly recommended and will be accounted in future publications. It started with nothing and it has materialized in something is the greatest satisfaction.

Prof. Dr. V. S. Patil

1

Galileo Galilei

At Pisa cathedral, a young medical student was kneeling for prayers. There was silence all over except annoying rattle of a chain. The chain was of a hanging lamp and some one just filled the lamp with oil and left. The tick-tack of the swinging chain interrupted that student and a chain of thoughts moved through his mind. He suddenly jumped up and it was great amazement for other worshippers and devotees. The idea that struck to the mind of the student was about the rhythm of the swinging lamp and it was regular! The pendulum of the rattling chain was taking exactly the same time for each of its oscillations, through the distances swept by oscillations, though the distance swept by oscillations was slowly becoming less and less. He rushed to his home and with the help of his friend he performed experiments with two pendulums. He noticed that the lengths of the pendulums were same but their oscillations were covering different distances (span of

sweep), still the time required for oscillation was same. Thus he discovered the great truths of the nature—the rhythmic principle and verified. Student was nothing but GALILEO!!

Galileo is the founder of modern science and modern scientific method. He was genius and had very versatile personality. He had such a wonderful qualities with him that one can astonished to know them. He was mathematician, musician, painter, eloquent speaker and debater, craftsman, thinker and philosopher, eminent teacher, master of Greek and Latin Languages, poet and writer, gardener, minute observer and interpreter of the highest order and highly skilled experimenter. He believed in 'truth and verified truth' only. He had courage to fight for the establishment of truth and break shackles of old traditions and customs. He was the creator of novel and great ideas. But at the same time he was ready to accept the idea only if it is verified by experiments and observations. He was the great scientists of 16th century. He was called 'the Archimedes of his day'. He loved and suffered lot for his convictions. He worked for the betterment of science with lot of torture and agony till his death. He used to believe as per Koran 'In heaven, the ink of scholar and the blood of martyr are of equal value'. Galileo had to face the fate of a scholar as well as a martyr.

His life is constant and everlasting source of motivation and inspiration for all the generations to come for the truth and pursuit of science. His life story is full of thrilling. His intellectual abilities are worth saluting. His satirical arguments were penetrating which caused many enemies. His arguments were for the truth and were irrespective of any person or a group. He boldly faced the consequences for his rebellion statements against established Aristotelian principles, catholic beliefs and Pope.

Galileo was born on 15th February 1564 at Pisa (Italy). His father Vincenzo Galilei was a great musician and mathematician. He inherited genius from his father. His mother, however was quarrelsome and satirical in nature. He was the eldest amongst the seven children of his parents. Incidentally he was born in the year when Shakespeare—the great poet and writer was also born. His financial position was not good throughout his life span. He had many debts and family responsibilities. He was good looking tall, handsome person with broad shoulders, red hairs, brilliance glittering in his eyes and hypnotic voice. He had many friends and foes as well. He never got married. He lived with Marina Gamba in one house and gave birth to three children—one son and two daughters. He believed that man can't be good, philosopher and a good husband. He had to spend a lot for the uplifting of his brothers and sisters. He remained controversial person, in his family and society. He believed in natural instinct and worked on mathematics as the language of nature. He was not happy as far as his family was concerned. He was exploited by his family members and died on 8th January 1642 in extreme agony. Incidentally, again in the same year Newton—one of the greatest scientists was born, Galileo's work also paved way for Newton's research.

Galileo was inquisitive and experimenting right from his childhood. He used to rely upon own senses and mind rather than the authority of others. His father referred him as star gazer, strange visionary and recipient of uncanny sounds. He used to construct crude little instruments and toys. Galileo entered University of Pisa as a student of medicine but then he left and became mathematician. During his days in Pisa, cathedral the incident cited in the beginning took place about 'the time of oscillation for pendulum' and he was just 17 years old! He used to cross question his teachers. It was quite abnormal in those days and now-a-days also this is not encouragable. It is assumed that all the issues were settled perfectly by great man, Aristotle once and for ever. The usual answer for his cross questions and arguments was – the master (Aristotle) had spoken (reference Magister Dixit –'The master has spoken'). In fact he wanted to learn the religious order, then to become both cloth merchant or doctor but none happened and he became mathematician and joined University of Pisa at the salary of 60 scudi a year.

Galileo kept on experimenting with pieces of string and lumps of lead, leavers, circles, angles and planes. He used these to solve the mysteries of the world. Galileo had asserted that two different weights released simultaneously from the same height would fall to the ground at the same time. It was contrary to the teachings of Aristotle. The professors at University also were of Aristotle's views. They challenged Galileo to prove his views and he accepted happily. The famous story of dropping the two weights one of ten pounds and the other of one pound from the top of Leaning Tower of Pisa (1591). The outcome was witnessed by professors, students and large audience from the town with lot of curiosity and anxiety. Galileo could prove his theory. Interestingly, though it was eye witnessed some professors still pretended that Galileo was wrong! It was surprisingly shocking.

Galileo was unconventional in teaching and living. It was convention to wear the robes (Gown and hood) for professors in classroom and outside too! Galileo disobeyed this rule and he insisted that robes interfered his free moments and the rule was ridiculous. There was therefore large opposition for him at the University campus and at King's level. Prince Don Giovamo De Medics had invented a dredging machine and it was suppose to be used for cleaning of Leghorn. A model of the machine was sent to Galileo for examination and report about its workability. Galileo's report was unfavourable but was objective and correct. He reported, the machine, was quite ingenious but with one drawback – it couldn't work. This was not palatable and as a result Galileo had to leave University of Pisa. He was at Pisa during 1589 to 1591. He then joined University of Padua in 1592 and remained there for 18 years.

Galileo's talent covered wide range of achievements – from the courses of stars to the manoeuvres of battle field, military architecture. Galileo earned name, fame and wealth (but he had many debts too) at Venice. Venice was a city of free thinking, frank living and jubilant laughter – much to the tune with Galileo's likings. At this city many of his discoveries and inventions were received with loud applause. He was always in contact with princes, nobles, soldiers and large number of admiring and devoting pupils. His inventions and discoveries include pendulum, pendulum clock, magnet and magnetic forces of earth, intricate compass a machine designed to raise water and irrigate the soil, crude slide rule, air thermometer, hydrostatic balance and the most amazing invention – the scientific telescope (1610).

The credit of discovering telescope goes to Dutch optician – Hans Lipperhey. He used to work with spectacle lenses in his shop – polishing glasses and combining them, He found that by placing a convex and concave lenses together – the system worked like telescope – which could make distance objects nearer and quite large. Galileo with his intellect, hard work and mathematical talent went on with Han's ideas and prepared first scientific telescope. It had magnifying power up to 33. The telescope was demonstrated to the public and was referred to as magic magnifying glass. People could see sails and ships far off the shore, cattle grazing on the distant hillside and worshippers going to churches in far away towns and villages. The most striking point of Galileo was, he turned the telescope from the earth surface to the sky and looked for distant stars and planets. This was the beginning of modern astronomy. He could see mountains and valleys on the surface of moon, Rings of Saturn, waxing and waning (phases) of Venice, 4 moons of Jupiter (now the number of moons of Jupiter is 12) and big red patch on it, the dark patches of sun, large number of stars in milky way. He also was of the opinion of Copernicus (Sun centred planetary systems/universe) and not earth centred universe as said by Ptolemy.

Telescope brought him great fortune but Galileo was interested to get back to his motherland Florence (and Pisa) from where he was removed with disgrace. He wrote 'The wings of fortune are swift but the wings of hope are drooping', this was his agony. He repeatedly requested Cosimo De Medici – the Grand Duke of Florence (and Pisa) to have him as a mathematician in his court but it could not happen. When Cosimo–II , the son of Cosimo I (and Galileo's pupil) came to throne he offered the position to Galileo in Florence and which resulted in tragic span of his later life.

Galileo's contribution to science is enormous. Apart from his celestial and terrestrial studies, he brought up machines as important branch of science. He tried to combine experimental observations with calculations to frame a theory.

He studied falling bodies, equilibrium and motion on inclined plane, motion of projectile and what not. He could get the centre of gravity by simple technique of hanging the figure through different points and get the intersection to perpendicular lines. His worked proved to be the base work for a great scientist Newton. Also William Harvey was able to study blood circulation in better way. He could prepare ancestor of slide rule (crude) to get the calculations done easily and quickly. He tried to formulate laws of motion. He wrote many books like – The Messenger of the Stars, The Laws of Motion, Dialogue Concern to New Science, Dialogue Concerning to System, The Solar Spots and The nature of

Comets, He wrote his greatest book 'The Laws of Motion' in prison at Arcetri. It was written in secret and smuggled to Holland for publication. Galileo never saw printed copy of the book because he became blind in the prison but could feel the pleasure of touch of the book and remarked 'I esteem this the most of all my works as it is outcome of my extreme agony' Poetically it is said "the greatest songs are those which tell us the saddest thoughts" He had to face a lot of torture by religious people, hypocrites learned and subjective administrations. He had such a conscious that could hardly be changed by pressures and earthly pleasures. His principles never changed under pressure or earthly pleasures, it remained always rebel and in tune with truth. He found out the method to get the weight of the object drowned under water. He could prove that air had a weight.

Galileo had a command on a language in which he used to express. He was witty and sarcastic. He used to defeat the opponents in discussion with intellectual arguments and logical presentations. He was hypnotic teacher and could get large followers of students from different sections of society. He used to mix with students and enjoy the cordial life with them. This was also not acceptable then. He was gifted writer and his writings also got good acceptance all over.

Galileo was strong supporter of Copernicus. However, he was well aware of the tragic burning of Bruna by religious authorities for his scientific declarations in support of Copernicus. Therefore, he did not write in his letters or books. His one observation – "I have observed that the earth too, moves around the sun". He merely mentioned it to some of his liberal friends. Irrespective of the fact, the Inquisition ruled with unlimited power and unflagging watchfulness. The Grand Inquisitor, Cardial Bellarmine had noted the views of Galileo. He asked Galileo to sign the declaration and to "abandon his heretical opinions about the earth and the sun and the stars" Galileo did "it" with death in his soul.

Cardial thus with a single decree had stopped the planets from moving around the sun. In long run however Galileo was unable to stifle his thoughts, as genius was born to express. As a result he was summoned to appear before Inquisition. Though Galileo was ill, he was relentlessly brought to Rome and when he was arrived there he was more dead than alive. The Inquisition was as unpopular as it was powerful. It had 'its way' Galileo had to write "... I now declare and swear that the earth does not move around sun" On June 22,1633, the friends then led him trembling and exhausted away from the tribunal. Galileo is said to have remarked under his breath "*Eppur si muove*" – But the earth does move!

Galileo was sentenced to prison at Arcetri. He became blind but he continued with his pursuits. Galileo's ideas got the large support but he had to suffer and surrender before power. Such is the drastic and heart moving story of the life of this great rare genius! It will linger and inspire the young minds of generations to come in pursuit of new ideas based on scientific methods and experimental verifications.

2

Alexander Van Humboldt

Alexander Van Humboldt was born on 14th September 1769 at Berlin and lived long life of about 90 years. He died in Berlin on 6th may 1859. During his life he travelled a lot. There were two major expeditions; one was in south-central America. He covered about 6000 miles distance walking, horse back or in canoes. The second expedition was in Russia and Siberia. The distance covered was about 11000 miles. More striking feature of second expedition was undertaken by Humboldt after the age of sixty with the same curiosity and enthusiasm of young creative scientist. After first expedition he spent his time in Paris for analyzing, interpreting and compiling specimens collected. He took help of many renowned men in scientific field for this work. He had published about 30 volumes consisting of 12000 pages. After his second expedition he was engaged in writing greatly admired gigantic work—'The Cosmos (Kosmos)'. It was published in 5 volumes (1845-1862). Four volumes were published in his life time and the last was published after his death. The

most important feature of his life was whatever he did was self sponsored. He bear all expenses of the expeditions and publications. He also helped to lot many budding young scientists like German chemist Liebig and Swiss Zoologist Lois Agassiz. From his early childhood he decided to devote his life to travel and study the world and its wonders. Indeed he did this till his death. He remained student for life since he had insatiable trust for knowledge. The students of University of Berlin had noticed "a small, white haired, old and happy looking man, dressed in a long brown coat, on the fifth bench near the window and taking notes." He was Alexander Van Humboldt. Whenever he was absent from the lecture room the students used to whisper "Alexander had bunk the class today to take tea with king." Such was the "The king of Science"—an ideal student. Similar to Nobel Prize in scientific field and peace fellowship named as "Humboldt Fellowship" is the most prestigious studentship for which world wide students aspire for.

Humboldt was the son of Major Van Humboldt, chamberlain to Frederick the Great. His mother belonged to French Protestants. He had one brother William. William was also a great man. He was a brilliant student of language studies. He brought reforms in Prussian educational system and founded University of Berlin (1807). Alexander used to remark about William that he is more clever than him and a real teacher. Major Van Humboldt died earlier and their mother was responsible for their upbringing. Alexander was privately educated. He studied political history and economics along with classics, languages and mathematics. His mother wanted him to be versatile. As a student he was poor. He had no interest in Army to which his father had likings. He studied Economics in the University of Frankfurt, then he wanted to study engineering in Berlin but noticed that he had strong aptitude for Botany. He tried to study the flora in the province of Brandenburg in Prussian Kingdom. He then joined University of Gottingen (1789-1790) for study the Mineralogy and Geology. Then he joined school of mines Freiburg. He then worked in mining department to explore Gold and Copper minerals (1792). He had varied experience of learning. He however could not be highly educated in a conventional sense.

His talent was nourished in early age by his father's library and nice garden around his house with multitudes of plants and shrubs. He had inculcated strong desire to read the book of nature and that of world. He had violent passion for travel beyond distant seas, even though the country to which he belonged had no navy and colonial possessions. His passion came to reality. The purpose of his explorations was to study the meaning of man in the mystery of nature. Humboldt's quest for knowledge was unparallel. He was conqueror of human ignorance. He fought for peaceful battle throughout his life. His life will be inspiration for all future naturalists. He is the idol for all thoughtful, daring and aspiring men. He had a body of adventurer and mind of scholar. Goethe had remarked about him. "He is like fountain with many pipes, you need only to get vessel to hold under it and on any side refreshing stream flew at a mere touch." He was thus the one man institution. He had wit and versatility. He surpassed in his qualities far ahead to that of '*Birbal and Chanakya*'. His gigantic work was such a monumental that many places in America and other are named after him. Humboldt Glacier, Humboldt river, Humboldt lake, Humboldt (Peru) current in Pacific ocean, Humboldt streets – town, university. He used to refer him as half American, Goethe had to further remark about him as a genius without rival in extent of information and acquaintances with existing sciences. He had encyclopaedic knowledge.

The King of Prussia used to get his advice because of his practical skills in diplomacy. Scholars admired him for his extraordinary genius. There was hardly any field literary, political, social movements on which his guidance was not taken. Geographers referred him for his first hand knowledge of expeditions. World over economists were aware of his deep insight of fiscal system of Germany. Many creative people used to visit him to kindle their own talent at the flames of his poetical inspiration. He had great insight about the history and meanings of words. Yet, he was modest above all. His daily routine in late ages reflected this fact. He used to examine his notes in the morning, in the afternoon he used to entertain the visitors who worshipped him and discuss with, in the evening he used to dine with the great king and in the night he used to write!!

Humboldt was an explorer and a scientist. He had pioneering work in earth sciences – Geography, Geology, and Geomagnetism. He was responsible for laying the corner stone of climatology—relation of plants and animals to their physiological surroundings. *i.e.* Ecology. He also studied volcanoes and earthquakes. He concluded that these were due to geological faults. He travelled many spots which were rarely witnessed by outsider and exhaustively studied them. During his expeditions, he had to put his life to utmost dangers and many times rumours about his death were received at Berlin and his friend's places. He was one of the earlier scientists to put the scientific data in graphic form. He drew isotherms—lines joining the points of equal average pressures on the map. He studied millions of specimens- flora, fauna, minerals, fossils etc. He had the richest collection of these specimens. He originated the concept of life zones—land area with uniform climate, soil and biota show, high degree of uniformity in species composition and adaptations to environment. He was the first observer to note that the temperature decreased as the height increased above the sea level. He saw many peaks of mountains and volcanoes. He could ascent Chimborazo (20561 feet altitude) up to the height of 19280 feet. It was record for next 30 years. He also noticed that the mountain illness was due to less proportion of Oxygen in the air. He sailed to America in 1804 and gave President Jefferson lot of information. Jefferson also was a scientist and could appreciate Humboldt's work more than anybody else. He was also responsible for popularizing science. In 1828 he organized first international conference of scientists in altogether difficult atmosphere politically. It was possible because he was looked upon in society as "the high priest" of intellectual world. His range of intellects was far wide and he used to dominate every discussion, conference and meeting easily and informally. He was like an elephant who could with equal ease tear down an oak tree or pick up a pin. He was therefore appointed to the Privy Council of the King of Persia and addressed thereafter—'His Excellency the Baron Van Humboldt'. He had human touch and his work about slavery and its removal remained concealed due to his other great achievements. He was born with silver spoon in mouth but throughout his life he tried to collect spoonful of information bit by bit leading to a large hoard. His work involved physical exertion and mental concentration. The following glimpses in his exploration can give an idea about his tedious and untiring work.

He got permission from the Spanish government to visit Spanish colonies in central and South America. In summer of 1799 he set sail accompanied by a French Botanist A. Bonpland. They travelled from 1799-1804 in central and south America. The name of ship they used was Pizarro. The two scientists made their way through sea, deep pathless forests and rivers. They entered the caves in pathless forests and rivers. They entered the caves in which South American night birds made their nests. These caves were believed to house the spirits of dead by natives. They needed to protect themselves from native's attack. They examined the curious plant of the dragon blood whose white bark was stained with its purple juice.

In Caracas they found paradise of coffee trees sugar canes. Next they explored the wilderness of the Amazon and noted cow trees. These trees gave geysers of milk. They rode through stagnant pools alive with electric eels. They were passing through death jaw. They took excursions along with rivers whose sandy banks were full of crocodiles lying motionless and with open jaws. Every year large number of the natives disappeared through river Orinoco by hired boat. During their night camps they had to lit a fire to keep away tigers and other wild animals.

Humboldt noticed the native tribes and their striking similarity in the customs and traditions. The underlying unity was 'All life is one'. He further explored area of Amazon and Rig Negro (rivers) batting poisonous insects. He found that natives made meals on white ants and on termites roasted in paste. There were omnivorous tribes whose diet extended not only to insects but to human flesh also. One of the Indians in Humboldt's canoe casually remarked that he was cannibal. He tried to explain the delicacy of the human palm as the food and that of bear palm too! There were different types of tribes and thrilling experiences. From south America he had travelled to Cuba and Mexico.

At the invitation of Russian Czar he set out on a scientific journey to the Ural Mountains, Mongolia, Caspian and Siberia and settled down in Berlin.

These journeys were not at all pleasure trips but they were heart breaking and life-death experiences – now and then. It was the tenacity and endurance of Humboldt that could make them possible.

Moreover Humboldt was with healthy association with great people of the world. He could utilize their expertise for compilation of his experiences. The examples are Gay Lussac—chemist, Arago-astronomer, Latreille, Cuvier-anatomists, Laplace-mathematician Vanqualin and Waproth—mineralogists and Bonpland and Kunth—Botanists.

He used to meet many great people and with warm clasp of shake hand. These personages include Frederick the Great, Schiller, Napoleon Bonaparte, William Pitt, Goethe, Thomas Jefferson, Alexander Hamilton, Walter Scott, Washington Irving etc.

He lived for about ninety years but before his ninetieth birthday he had to go for still another voyage but not to return.

3

Gregor Johann Mendel

Mendel, father of the Genetics Science, was born at the Moravian Village of Heinzendorf on July 22, 1822. In Austrian Silesia, Heinzendorf was known as 'the flower of Danube' Mendel's love for nature was inherited from several generations of peasants and gardeners. He was brought up in a surrounding with a passion for growing things. His father was a peasant and had a special liking for horticulture. Mendel passed major part of his childhood tending the plants in his father's garden. Fortunately in his elementary schooling at Heinzendorf the study of nature was also the part of curriculum. The roots of Mendel's future development as a natural scientist are found in his early schooling. Mendel went for high school learning in the neighbouring town of Troppau. He was quite poor and during his high school days of six years he was partly starving. As a result of privations he fell seriously ill in 1839 and was compelled to interrupt his studies.

One winter day while his father was chopping the tree, the trunk fell upon his chest and partially crushed it. His father could not therefore go to farm and he sold the farm. The sum gained thus was turned to Johann Mendel. Johann continued his study of philosophy at the Olmutz Institute. He studied for four years in the institute devotedly and with lot of trouble and tenacity. During his days at Olmutz, he occasionally suffered illness and perpetual hunger. Prof. Michael Franz advised him to join a monastic life. As a result Mendel entered the Augustinian monastery at Altbrunn and assumed the name of Gregor.

There was nice and spacious botanical garden on the monastery grounds. It was developed by father Thaler. Thaler was noted botanist known for his profound learning and spiritual fervours. Father Thaler however was in the habit of following up a hard day in the garden with a merry evening at the tavern with liberal wine cup. It was not liked by the abbot of the monastery—father Cyril Napp. Thaler left the monastery leaving behind the memory of his pleasant personality and also the legacy of a well stocked and scientifically cultivated garden. This garden was God given gift for Mendel. He spent all his spare moments in this garden, "watching and nursing the plants from their infancy to their old age" There were many monks of this type. They shared the joy of tending the plants and in their evenings they discussed theology, literature, philosophy, science and occasionally politics even. Those were the revolutionary days of the eighteen forties. Such currents also affected Mendel and for same time he served as a parish priest. He could not withstand the sight of sufferings. He was a student rather than fighter. He was too sensitive then and returned to monastery.

He worked in the garden also, but his temperament was too energetic and he craved for more assignment. He had a liking for instructions and applied for a position as substitute teacher in the local high school. He got the job and his work was quite satisfactory (1849). People in authority concluded that he was competent enough to server as a permanent teacher. The examiners who were authorized to qualify him as a permanent teacher could not pass him twice on account that "he has not mastered this subject sufficiently". Such was the verdict of the then 'experts' on scientific ability of one of history's great scientists. Mendel's failure (1850) in those examinations was due to his originality'. It was not palatable to his examiners, they grudged—"This candidate pays no attention to technical terminology. He uses his own words and expresses his own ideas instead of relying upon traditional knowledge". Mendel remained different and original. Mendel had that reputation—for generations—a stubborn and tenacious stock. They fought with guns and insisted on their rights. They were reluctant to go with others wills and wishes arbitrarily. It remained in his blood to select own course of action, think independently and to pursue it to the end irrespective of all opposition or even failures.

Mendel was sent to University of Vienna during 1851-1853 to study physics, chemistry, mathematics, botany and zoology. He taught at Brunn/Brno which is in Moravia a part of Czechoslovakia, in a technical high school for quite long time. i.e. 1854-1868. He was a nice teacher. He used to make his lectures interesting by telling his experiences and anecdotes through he lacked formal training, Mendel's teaching did not interfere with his duties—monastic and garden tending. He was happy short and stocky little fellow. He had high forehead, a wide and generous mouth, a healthy appetite, healthy laugh and gray blue eyes with a twinkle of cordial good will. He was contented spirit with a beautiful world around. During the course Brunn also experienced the evil of Prussian invasion (1866) and later he could work undisturbed. He became Abbot in 1868.

Mendel was interested in the cross fertilization of common pea—*Pisum Satirum*. Mendel hoped that—"Out of the simplest things we shall know the truth. I am convinced that inheritance takes place according to definite laws or principles." He tried to find these laws, he got the little plot of the land in the monastery garden and transformed it into a living text book. He selected twenty two varieties of the edible pea with different shape, size, colour and texture of the skin of seed wrinkled or smooth. He carefully noted the characteristics of their 'children or offspring'. He did his monumental work during 1856-63—8 years. He studied around 28000 plants.

The summary of the characteristics discovered by Mendel in the successive generations can be briefly put as follows:

1. When two different types of plants or of animals are mated all the offspring of the generation will be a like. It is called 'the law of uniformity'. For example—

   (*a*) If you cross a red flower with white flower all the offspring will be gray.

   (*b*) If you cross horse with ass, offspring will be mule. Mule is called hybrid.

2. When the uniform offspring will of the different plants are mated, the resultant offspring will not be uniform, but will segregate themselves into different forms according to a definite numerical ratio. This is called 'the law of segregation' For example—

   (*a*) If you cross grey flowers that have sprung from the crossing of red flower and white flower, you will get the following results. Out of every eight offspring, two will be red, two will be white and four will be grey. The crossing of the red flowers of this generation will always produce 'red flowers'. The crossing of white flowers of this generation will always produce 'white flowers'. But the crossing of the grey flowers of this generation will out of every eight offspring produce 'two red flowers, two white flowers and four grey flowers'. These in turn will follow the same rule further. The production from grey generation will be always in the ratio 1:2:1. This law of proportional segregation will hold true of every successive generation of 'inter marriage' or 'cross breeding' of plants or of animals or of human beings.

   (*b*) Let us illustrate with second example. Let us cross breed 'tall' variety with 'dwarf' variety. The first generation F, will be hybrid tall variety. The second generation from hybrid tall variety will result 25% pure tall variety, 50% hybrid tall variety and 25% pure dwarf variety (F2). It is in the ratio 1:2:1.

3. In above two cases the dominance if the properties is assumed equally. But in many cases dominance of one is more than the other. The other is referred as recessive character. Then the 'law of independent assortment' holds good. The ratio then becomes 3:1 and not 1:2:1. In the next generation it will be 9:3:3:1 and not 2:6:6:2.

Mendel studied paired elementary units of heredity. They are now known as genes. In peas 7 pairs were studied. Recent advances in this field have proved that heredity characters are associated with DNA—Deoxyribonucleic acid. The structure of DNA was established by Watson and Crick. It is proved to be double stranded α helix. They got the Nobel prize in chemistry (1954) for their important discovery and explanations of heredity thereby.

He read his paper on 'Experiments on Plant Hybridization'—'*Weruche isner pfianzinnhybriden*' for the first time on 8th February 1865 before the Altbrunan society for the study of Natural Science. His audience listened politely, applauded faintly and promptly forgets the whole thing. Mendel took 7 to 8 years of patient research to find it all out. Audience report was quite disheartening—'Eight years spent in watering ordinary pea plants grow what a waste of time.' He published his papers in proceedings of the natural science society of Brunn in 1865 and 1866. His work lay neglected on the dusty shelves of a few libraries. With this universal apathy toward his scientific efforts, he went back to his monastic duties and teachings. The world took more than 30 years to realize the greatness of his work. It was in 1900, due to the work of three scientists, Mendel came to lime light. They were Hugo de Vries—the Dutch Botanist, Karl Correns—German Biologist and Erich Tschermark—Austrian scientist. William Baterson—English scientist also upheld the views. Mendel got the reorganisation as 'Father of Science of Genetics'.

Mendel selected simple pea plant for his studies because it is self pollinating petals enfold and protect its reproductive organs from wind and insects. This prevents the pollen of other flowers from entering and affecting fertilization. He also tried other route. He opened the immature bud, removed the stamens and deposited pollen from another plant upon 'its intact' pistils. At the advise of Nageli from University of Munich, Mendel carried out some experiments with Heiracium (Hockweed) plant and on honey bees. These experiments were not that successful. In Heiracium plant the embryo is formed from the ovum without fertilization (parthenogenesis), may be the reason. In scientific pursuits these things are common. Mendel's laws of uniformity, segregation and independent assortment are well established and heredity is explained in the most fundamental way and simple too! Blood is nothing to do with heredity as it is commonly talked about. It is more or less a phrase! It is also known that heredities do not mix but they are segregated.

Mendel was quite popular as a teacher. Pupils used to come to his classes eagerly to imbibe his knowledge and especially for the pleasure of acquiring the same. Pupils used to chuckle over his anecdotes. They learnt lot about his 'children'—the plants, the insects and the animals in his garden. He frequently invited his pupils into the monastery to acquaint them with the habits and behaviour of plants, bees, birds, mice etc. It was the live experience of learning. Whenever circus came to town, he took entire class to circus and had interactions with animals and birds in circus. It was a sort of chat with animals. It was just like reading the book of nature. His pupils admired his good natured humours towards his own mistakes even! Most of the people respected his gentleness. His impartial smile was shared with both the types of students. The brilliant, accepted it as a compliment whereas the stupid, accepted it as an encouragement. He had all grief of his own failures in his examinations to quality as a permanent teacher, he rarely allowed any of his pupils to suffer a set back. The weak students were invited to the monastery garden for special tuition without pay. He made learning interesting. Mendel himself was highly motivated by the book of Charles Darwin—origin of species. He educated many students. His sister Theresia gave her amount due to Mendel for his education in his earlier days. He took entire responsibility of her three sons and born the expenses of their high school and college training. He was lavish with his purse even to the strangers. He was spontaneous in giving rather than receiving. He believed the beneficiary by advertising yourself as his benefactor.

He had to taste the bitter fruits of unpopularity in his later life. He however, remained firma and rather obstinate. In the opinion of many of his acquaintances, he was ill advised. The issue was about 'the taxation of church property'. The bill was passed to increase the taxes. Mendel regarded this bill as unconstitutional and refused to pay the tax on the monastery at Altbrunn. He sent 'voluntary contribution' to the state treasury accepting the fact that an increase in the Moravian religions fund was necessary. The state refused to accept the contribution and Mendel refused to pay the tax. The struggle went on for several years. The government tried to persuade him on one side and threaten him on the other side. He was 'lonely crusader struggling for the right'; the state looked upon him as 'foolish old man who refuses to obey the law.' The struggle remained undecided. Mendel started suffering from pathological irritability. He was hopeful that he could see in his life time the 'obnoxious law' revoked. It was not to happen. In the spring of 1883 he suffered a heart attack. He could recover partially and spent some time with his birds, plants, animals and bees; still experimenting with the laws of life through he know that his own life was at an end.

The end came on January 6, 1884. People mourned the passing of a lovable but rather obstinate old clergyman and popular teacher. But none of the mourners could be able to realize that a supreme scientist and father of science of genetics had just passed forever.

With recent advances in the field like 'Cloning of ship: Dolly' by Wilmut and his team, the work of Mendel is emphasized more and more.

4

Thomas Alva Edison

Edison was technological genius. His role in taming science for comforts of human being was unique. He was referred as 'The Electric Thomas Edison.' In his long life of eighty four years he had as large as 1093 patent at his credit. Most of his work was carried out at a place called 'Menlo Park.' He was known to the world as the wizard of 'Menlo Park.' He was a kind of legend—the miracle man of the technical age. He worked almost eighteen to twenty hours a day throughout his life. He applied his immense energy, brilliant capacities and soaring imagination to innumerable technical and scientific ideas. He had three important qualities—imagination, optimism and self confidence. He had unlimited patience and very high capacity to hard work. His famous definition of genius is worth remembering—"Genius is 1% inspiration and 99% perspiration." He was humble and witty. Many a times he was just plain, mischievous. He had nice appearance and pleasant face, though he used to dress carelessly and with number of signs of chemicals and hard work. He was the most popular American living

personalities. Before his death, American newspapers conducted polls to determine the ten greatest living Americans. There was considerable difference of opinion about the lists, but each pole agreed that the greatest of all was Thomas Alva Edison. His life was fascinating and interesting. It could inculcate enterprising spirit and the message—'Work is Worship.' His successes are well known but he knew failures also frequently. He never hesitated out of fear of failure. He would tell discouraged co-workers during trying services of experiments. "We haven't failed. We now know 1000 things that won't work, so we are that much closer to finding what will. " It is said—'Not failure but low aim is crime' It is seen in the life of Edison and so he will be ever remembered as 'Yes' man.

The Edison had been rebels and pig headed self made men for generations. They come from Holland. They carried Fishermen's hearts for 'any fate' and unfathomable will to explore as sea! Thomas Alva Edison's father was Samuel Edison and mother Nancy—school teacher. His mother came from family of American revolutionaries. To this distinguished parent Alva was born on 11th February 1847 at little town Milan by shore of Lake Erie. He was proved to be realization of American dream from 'rags to riches' through hard work and native intelligence. He became folk hero to his fellow countrymen. His father moved to Port Huron for grain business. Alva was seven then and was admitted to Port Huron public school. As a student, Alva was rated as 'addled'. He paid little attention to the books and kept asking series of questions, both at school and at home. Curiosity was his dominant trait therefore teacher would not like Alva. Alva's mother was bold and rushed to school teacher and told— "Well, if anybody here is addled it's you. You could call yourself lucky if you had half as much brain as Alva and mark my words" she added, 'some day the world will hear of him—but never of you!' This ended Alva's formal school education which lasted only for three months. She taught Alva. Alva wrote years later, 'My mother was the making of me. She instilled in me the love and purpose of learning'. Mother was his motivating force. He read a lot at young age and experimented in a laboratory at the basement of the house. This was continued till he was twelve.

Then he took a job in railway shuttling from Port Huron to Detroit. His headquarters was the luggage van. In this van he kept papers, sweets and candies, vegetables, chemicals and books. He was the newspaper boy. In between, he used to experiment and read. He started in the same luggage car, his own paper—The Weekly Herald. He was writer, printer, salesman, editor etc. He was whole and sole of the paper—one man institute. He was just 15 then. The famous tragic incidence took place on this train journey once. At the sharp curve, a stick of phosphorous fall on the floor, from Al's laboratory shelf and at once caught fire. The conductor rushed into the van and threw all things out and gave Alva a formidable box on the left ear. It is said to be the reason for his deafness. Some reports have alternate reasons. Once, Thomas was to enter the van with both hands full of luggage when conductor tried to get him in by pulling his ears. This resulted in deafness. Whatever be the reason this great man was deaf. He never invented hearing and used to say in support of this like "A man who has to shout can never tell a lie." He was truthful deaf man. This accident ended his career in the newspaper world.

Once he was on the platform of Mount Clemens Station watching the fascinating spectacle of shunting. A small child was saved from crashing under fright truck by him. Instantly, it gave turn to his career. That child was son of station master. In gratitude the station master could teach Edison telegraphy. Telegraphy was relatively a new thing. Only eighteen years ago the first experimental line had been opened between Washington and Baltimore by the inventor, Samuel Morse. He learnt Morse mysterious code of dots and dashes for the purpose. He however had an experience of his own telegraphy in between his house and that of friend's at Port Huron. He was then offered the job of a telegraph operator on the Grand Trunk line, when he was 16. He made his first invention there. Night operator needed to send a message after every hour in a form of a signal. Edison devised an automatic clock and a wheel with notched rim which could do job of sending message for him. He worked for number of companies as telegraph operator for 5 years. During the time he also kept on experimenting with chemicals. There was another accident by him. He upset a carboy of sulfuric acid in the telegraph room and acid leaked in the manager's office below. He was removed from that office and then he joined Boston. There he was recognized as fastest and exact telegraph operator.

He used to keep him busy awfully. He had to do many things. He read Faraday's experiments and repeated many of them. He could hardly sleep. He used to work till he could automatically get a nap and could eat whenever he felt quite hungry. He maintained—"Sleep is like a drug. Take too much at a time and it makes you dopey. You lose time, vitality and also opportunities" Soon he built a working model of the first invention for which he took out a patent. It was 'Vote recorder' He went to Washington to demonstrate his invention to a Committee of House of Representatives. The machine was quick and remarkable but it was not required that way by politicians. Edison took a lesson out of this and decided not to invent something for which there was no demand. 'Need based activity' then became his motto. He remained practical and utility oriented throughout his life.

He then got a job in Gold Indicator company at New York. It was very big company around famous Wall Street and Mr. Laws owned it. In that company once the transmitter of the gold-reporting telegraph was not working. No body could repair it. Edison did the settling of the transmitter without much difficulty and became technical manger, at the salary of $300a month. It was big money for him but he was never interested in money. He used money to achieve more and more in scientific and technological fields. For him money was a means but not an end. Mr Laws sold the company to General Lefferts—Gold and Stock Telegraph Company. In that company he invented entirely new machine—the Edison Universal printer for which he took out a patent and sold to Lefferts for 40000 dollars (1870). During next five years he worked with inventions and innovations connected with telegraphy. In his new laboratories at Newark he could send two or even four telegrams through same wire. Many people were trained in his laboratories. He believed in 'group or team work'.

Edison married with Mary Stilwell (1871) when he was 24. Mary was engaged as research worker at the Edison's laboratories and she was a capable and valuable assistant to him. His father Samuel searched a new place for his laboratories at 'Menlo Park'. They shifted there in 1876 with two children Dot and Dash, as Alva used to call them instead of Marion and Thomas Junior.

The next instrument which excited Edison most was Bell's telephone. It was both receiver and transmitter. He tried to improve the quality of transmitted sound and devised the instrument called 'microphone' Recording of human voices, music and other sounds for further repetition was started with Edison in 1877. It was the first recorded sound of Edison—"Mary had a little lamb, its fleece was white as snow..." This invention made sensation—unparallel! It was 'phonograph' or 'talking machine'. This was the pet invention of Edison. It remained at back scene for 10 years and its improved version came in 1888 as 'gramophone'. Original form of phonograph was also called 'Ediphone or Dictaphone'

Edison then turned his attention to electric light. His idea was to produce 'glow' or 'incandescence' in a wire when electricity was passed through it. This 'glow' would be actual source of light. Edison's team of forty to fifty people worked with the idea endlessly. Thousands of glass bulbs were evacuated (made empty of air with vacuum pumps) so that the wire that can be stuffed in, would glow but not burn, when electric current passed through. They tried innumerable wires for the purpose and spent lot of money about 50000 dollars. Finally they succeeded with sewing thread. They placed the thread in muffle—furnace for five hours for carbonization. This carbonized thread was placed in evacuated glass bulb and sealed. Electric current was then passed through the thread which started glowing soft and yellow. Edison and his team stared at it with fascination. The electric lamp this produced could glow for over forty hours (1879)! This was the wonderful discovery by the wizard of Menlo Park. Edison invited everybody to see his electric lamps at Menlo Park on New Year's Eve—1880. Visitors were greeted with the glow of thousands of lamps strung along two wires on the road from the station to the laboratory. Whole district of New York became first electrically lit area on September 4, 1882. The electric age began with Edison's discovery of electric lamp.

Edison was also instrumental for the beginning of the great film industry. He built at his new laboratory in West Orange the first film studio in the world and named—'Black Maria'. He invented machines called Kinetograph and Kinetoscope which could exhibit a scene in motion with a phonograph playing music at background. Edison could do it on celluloid film in camera moving across the lens at constant speed.

There is one more incidence of fire worth recording here which indicates Edison's endurance and tenacity. It was the year 1914, and month December when fire took off in the plant of his laboratory. Spontaneous combustion occurred in the film room. It was disastrous fire. Edison was 67 that time. He took the incidence sportingly and called upon his wife and her friends to witness the 'rare' scene. He further announced—"We are rebuilding, all of our mistakes have been destroyed. We have just cleared out a bunch of old rubbish. In a new factory we can start our experiments with a clean slate."

After the outbreak of First World War he put himself to the disposal of U.S. Government. He worked for import substitutes for chemicals like phenol (carbolic acid), cresols, dyes and drugs. At the age of eighty he was involved in Botany. He never retired. He tried to search native source of rubber. He tested and classified 17000 varieties of plants. He could finally extract latex from the plant—golden rod, in substantial quantities. He recorded his work in note books. The numbers of note books thus prepared were 3400. It gives the idea about vast amount of work that he put in. He remarked about his achievements as "I owe my success to the fact that I never had a clock in my work room"

Because of his tremendous work schedule, his family life was relatively restricted. But he did find time to go fishing, motoring and the like with the family and to play games and romp on the floor with children. His first wife Mary died of typhoid in 1884. He dug himself yet deeper into his work—heart broken. He was fortunate enough to have beautiful Mina Miller as his second wife in 1886. Mina converted incorrigible, tobacco chewing eccentric Edison into presentable man in polite society. Mary had three children so also Mina. Mina's son Charles Edison was governor of New Jersey. Edison was friendly, candid and energetic. He had a face of dreamer and yet of a man of action. Physically he had broad shoulder and strong chest for hard work and endurance. His hands were muscular, long and sensitive. He received many medals and awards. One worth noting is special "Gold Medal of the Congress of United States" in 1928. His laboratory is well maintained by American Government as the national monument. His was all applied research and he set up industrial research laboratory. He however has theoretical contribution known as 'Edison Effect'. He left this discovery for others to develop while others were vice versa.

Edison died at the age of 84 at West Orange on 18th October 1931. On the day of his funeral all electric current in United States was to be cut off for one minute. This was deemed to be too costly and dangerous. Therefore, only certain lights were dimmed. The wheels of 'Continuity of work' were not stilled even for a fraction of a minute. Edison would have appreciated that way only.'

5 Dmitri Ivanovich Mendeleev

If one looks into the books preferably text books, involving some calculations, at the end one finds logarithmic tables. These tables are used for calculations giving quick answers. Now-a-days calculator are commonly used instead of these tables. Similarly if one goes into general chemistry or especially inorganic chemistry text books, one finds a table "Periodic Table of Elements" This table at a glance gives the gist of about hundred and seven elements. Table has number of rows called periods and number of columns called groups. The elements in the same group have similar properties and as you go from left to right in a row metallic characters changes gradually to non-metallic characters. For example in the first group metals like lithium, sodium and potassium are present. Metals are lustrous, heavy and conduct heat and electricity. They are malleable and ductile on the contrary in the seventh group non-metals are present. They include chlorine, bromine

and iodine. They are called halogen family characterized by lighter weight, non-conductors of heat, electricity and brittleness. This was the earlier classification of elements into metals and non-metals. Thus on the left, metals are found and on the right non-metals.

The name associated with excellent chemistry text books and periodic table is Dmitri Ivanovich Mendeleev. He was a Russian chemist. His father was a teacher. He was fourteenth child of the parents. The father had tough time and was very poor. Mendeleev was born on 7th February 1834 at Tabolsk in Siberia. Siberia was outside the academic pole of the country and those people were taken little backward and common. His father was teacher of Arts and Literature, he went blind earlier and when Dmitri was just 14 he died. His mother struggled a lot and ran a local glass factory. Unfortunately the factory got on fire just after one year of father's death. The brave mother moved with Dmitri Mendeleev and his sister (two dependent children) to St. Petersburg (now Leningrad). She tried to get admission for her son in University of St. Petersburg and also for medical education but in vain. She struggled a lot for education (pedagogical) course. He completed the course with flying colours and got Gold Medal in 1855. He was thus qualified for teacher's post. He was not at all good health-wise, he was suffering from tuberculosis. He has to complete his education with poor earnings of the family and basically on scholarships. He was posted at Odesa (Crimia) but continued with study of chemistry. In 1856 he took degree from St. Petersburg in chemistry and got appointment in University in 1857. At his early studentship he was good in mathematics, physics and geography but had in classic languages. He was sent by the Government to Heidelberg in 1859. He got in contact with many scientist there Bunsen and Kirchhoff were the two great scientist working at Weideberg and many young people use to seek their guidance for scientific pursuits. Mendeleev preferred to work independently. This was his characteristics features. He was however influenced by Italian chemist—S. Cannizarro's work. He found that there was no suitable text book in chemistry and devoted two years (1868-70) For preparing excellent text book in chemistry namely "Principles of Chemistry" The book was very well received and it was then translated into number of languages. It was his classic writing. During these days he studied the elements, their properties and periodic similarities in them. He formulated his law in 1869 which stressed that properties of element are periodic functions of their atomic weights. This was the most important organizing principle of chemical knowledge. This gave strong impetus to inorganic chemistry as that given by molecular structure to organic chemistry.

It is said that science is systematized body of knowledge. Classification therefore has importance in science. Logical and rational classification is foundation of Modern Science. Elements were earlier classified as metals and non-metals. The elaborate classification of elements by Mendeleev in periodic table is therefore landmark in the development of chemistry. In Mendeleev's days some 70 elements were known, 20 of them were non-metals. Majority of the rest were metals and quite few metalloids (in between metals and non metals in properties) Mendeleev observed that properties of elements repeat after some elements. When arranged according to their increasing atomic weights. Atomic weight is a average weight of atoms of elements for example sodium has similar properties with potassium. It is eighth element after sodium. Similar Beryllium – magnesium, Boron – Aluminium, carbon silicon, Nitrogen- phosphorus, Oxygen – Sulfur, Fluorine-Chlorine, show marked resemblance in their properties. This periodicity is universal in nature. In a year months are repeated, seasons are repeated. This arrangement of elements give host of information. In nut shell and makes it precise. Mendeleev's work therefore is monumental.

Mendeleev not only arranged the elements but also left some of the places in his table vacant, to be filled in future by the elements, These new elements indeed were discovered in a course of twenty years and occupied the expected places in periodic table. Their properties were very similar as forecasted by Mendeleev by their position in table, such was prophetic effect of the table and Mendeleev's genius. Any theory holds true if it can forecast correctly. The three elements thus predicted and discovered were Eka-boron (Scandium-1870) Eka Aluminium (Gallium 1875) and Eka Silicon (Germanium-1886) The names prefixed with Eka were given by Mendeleev and their properties were similar to prefixed elements. Thus Eka-Silicon *i.e.* Germanium has similar properties with Silicon. He could correct atomic weights of some elements on the basis of periodic table. Atomic weight of Beryllium was corrected from 14.9 to 9.0%. Periodic table proved to be awakening force for discovering new elements. Argon and Helium were inert gases known earlier Xenon and Krypton were the inert gases discovered by Ramsey on this basis. Mendeleev's periodic table has some drawbacks for example copper, silver and gold metals are placed in the same group as that of reactive metals like sodium and potassium, Though their properties were different (less reactive) where as mercury, lead and barium having similar properties were placed in different groups. There were some anamolous places if known earlier they would have got different places though their properties are very similar because of different atomic weights.

In following years new periodic law was discovered based on atomic number (number of protons in atom) and not an atomic weight. This happens. Good reasons of force should give place to better. This doesn't defy the importance of Mendeleev. He ranks equal position with theoretical chemists like A. Lavoisier who professed that an element is ultimate unit of matter and J. Dalton who concluded that all atoms of the element were identical and with measurable atomic weight.

Independent working with confidence was special feature of Mendeleev. Though Mendeleev is identified with periodic table he had large areas of work at his credit. He carried large number of experiments near Moscow in agriculture. Use of fertilizers, quality seeds and increased production were measure areas of work. These were novel ideas those days through they sound quite simple now. He improved upon Soda Industry in Russia. He visited places like France (Paris) and America. He studied petroleum industry critically. He revamped petroleum and oil strategies in Russia. Now it established that these industries are critical to keep nation ahead in progress. This industry has become turning point, basic issue and political centre world over. His studies also encompassed all together different types like aerodynamics (related to speed of aero planes).It is important subject from the point of Sputniks and space research. He improved the tariff procedure for imported heavy chemicals. His government placed him as the head of weights and measure department since 1893. He was awarded many medals and prizes like Davy Medal in 1882 and Copley Medal in 1905. His work was published in 25 volumes. Such was varied work of Mendeleev. His capacity was tremendous.

Mendeleev, however, had stormy personal life. His views were not in tune with Czar Government. He held progressive outlook and wanted to reform conservative outdated education system in Russia. He lead student's agitation for the purpose. He was forced to leave academic position in 1890. He was also not given membership of Imperial Academy of Sciences. Many attempts were done to tarnish his image and lower him down but his work was such a great and useful that government has to accept him as such and go ahead. He was also interested in social reform and was critic of political situation. His first marriage took place in 1863. It lasted for 13 years. It was the rule those days that after divorce one can't marry for 7 years. Mendeleev broke this rule and married with his Arts student before 7 years. Marriage was thus illegal. His stature was such a great that it could not be suppressed by rules and regulations of government. He had large followers in student community as a nice teacher and reputation of a scientist world over. Government could only deny some of the facilities and honours. Government could not do without him. He was thus indispensable irrespective of his anti views. It was always said about him that he was too useful to be left idle. Government however tried to harass him. It is worth noting that even though he was made to resign academic post in 1890. He was appointed head of weights and measure department in 1893.

Mendeleev was greatly admired for his monumental contribution one is periodic table and the other excellent text books. His work however covered large areas like chemistry, agriculture, climatology, mathematics etc. In his honour one element with atomic number 101 was named as Mendelevium. The element was discovered at California by a group of scientists headed by J. T. Seaborg. It is man made element obtained by atomic transmutation. It is radio active element. The stable isotope has mass 258. Its valency was 2 and 3.

Mendeleev will be ever remembered by all school going students to scientists for his periodic table scholarships, hard and tough time to early childhood. He was confidence, independent thinking, good teaching, poor health, stormy personal life and stubborn social and political views. He died of Pneumonia on 2nd February 1907 but is immortal due to periodic table.

Mendeleev was independent and worked in non-conventional way. Once he went high up with the help of balloon to perform some experiments and observations. People gathered in masses to see him. He stood up on platform suspended at the end of the balloon and cheered up and wished the people. If we recall this scene we realize Mendeleev's genius and great popularity. He used to face any trouble, agonies for doing convinced things and he will not leave it. Indepth study and observations were his peculiarities. Thus he was a rare individual.

6

Louis Pasteur

It is said—"Necessity is the mother of inventions". This is true for Louis Pasteur's research work. Pasteur was a French chemist and microbiologist. His contributions to science and industry are valued and varied. Applied and useful research for advancement of mankind was the significant point about his work. He is the first scientist to strengthen the university-industry relationship for the mutual benefits in search of knowledge and its application. Relevance of research was strong point in his contributions. He was fortunately able to get high esteem, celebrations, respect, regards and honours for his achievements from the people of France and all other countries. He was rated as the first man of choice by French people while the great Napoleon was rated as fifth. Such was the loud applause for him. Pasteur's farewell message to the world was "Science and peace will triumph over ignorance and war—in the long run the nations will learn to unite not for destruction but for cooperation—and that the

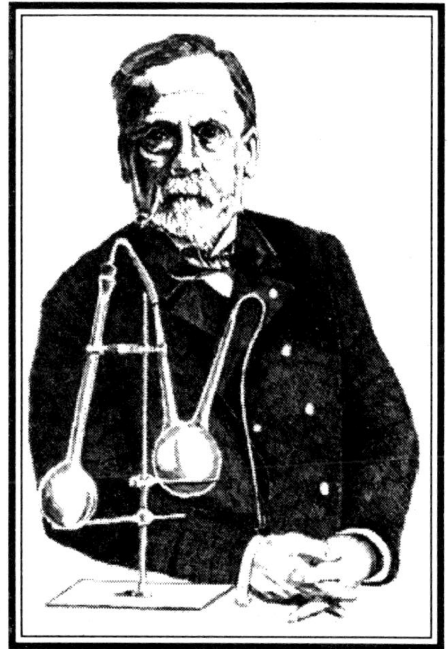

future will belong not to the conquerors but the saviours of mankind." Pasteur was thus a prophetic scientist.

Pasteur was born on 27th December 1822 at Dole. His father was a tanner and he got the smell of the leather in his blood. When he was placed at Ecole Normale in Paris for his studies, during those days his homesickness and the strong attraction for the smell was reflected. He was ill once there and no medicine but visit to home cured him. He completed his school in the village Arbois. He was quite an ordinary student. He however had insatiable curiosity, skilful experimental hand and remarkable gift of observation. His teacher once remarked about him "his business is not to *ask* the questions but to *answer* them". He answered many and most valuable questions during his life span. He was a patient worker. For him *will, work* and *wait* were the three most important words in the dictionary on which he built the towering pyramid of his success. Right from his childhood he had made up his mind to be a chemist making the transition from the smell of tannery to the odours of laboratory. He was highly motivated by the lectures of the great chemist Dumas. He remarked about Dumas as "Not only a scientist but a poet as well. He arouses the curiosity and kindles the imagination". His father believed in the virtues of his son and wrote 'We can't judge your essays but we can certainly judge your character. You have given us nothing but satisfaction'. Such was the admiring and patronizing father. His mother was also intelligent.

Pasteur was staunch nationalist. When the revolution of 1848 broke out, he sacrificed his savings and was ready to sacrifice his life too. He left his position and joined National Guard at the city of Orleans. He however could rejoin his scientific pursuits soon. After many years his son was also in the French Army and was survived crucially out of the war. It was the point of comfort in the sorrowful latter life of Pasteur. Pasteur was basically serious and sad. There was eternal sorrow in his life. He hated wars and aggressions. He returned his honorary Diploma of Doctor of Medicine received from the University of Bonn because of barbarity and hypocrisy of Kaiser Wilhelm (German), Kaiser was responsible for the massacre of two great nations (1870-71)

Pasteur got good education and doctor's degree. He joined Ecole Normale, Paris as laboratory assistant. He worked rigorously on crystallography for about ten years (1847-57). He worked on crystallizations of tartaric acid and sodium ammonium salts of tartaric acid. He studied the effect of one type of crystals in relation to other types of crystals in solution on plane polarized light. These two types of substances had all the properties identical except the effect on light. These crystals had object to mirror image relationship. One type rotated the plane of polarization to the right (dextro +) and the other to the left (laevo -). The detailed interpretations led the foundations of interesting and novel branch of Organic Chemistry i.e. Stereochemistry. The intricate structural arrangement of these substances in biological and medical fields was predicted. It is now established that many 'object' type of structures can cure diseases but 'mirror image' type of structures cannot. For example—Ephedrine [laevo(–)] is used in treatment of hay fever and bronchial asthma. (–) chloromycetin is effective in curing pneumonia, typhoid fever etc. Important constituent of thyroid glands is Thyroxine and is laevorotatory. These examples are just few to illustrate the importance of intricate structures on the biological and medical activities of substances. Pasteur's work in crystallizations and molecular asymmetry brought him good name and fame. He also got the professorship of chemistry at Strasbourg. He entered the other fields later on. He said "I wish I had a new life before me, for my studies on crystals".

At Strasbourg he could get his life partner. He was fortunate to have "friend, philosopher and guide" type wife. His wife had deep sense of understanding and devotion for Pasteur. His foresight and judgment about a lady chosen as wife was as acutely correct as in his research. It is an interesting story. Laurent was the rector of Stransbourg University. Marie Laurent was his daughter. Pasteur proposed to Marie and wrote to her father about the intention. He explained his background plainly and wrote "I have therefore no fortune. All that I possess is good health, good courage and my position in the University. I plan to devote my life to chemical research." The response for the letter was obviously unfavourable. Pasteur as usual was patient and hard working. He wrote to the mother now that "Marie Laurent should not prepare her mind on first impression. As the time passes people have liked me" and finally to Marie Laurent—"...time will show you that under this cold and shy exterior there is a heart full of affection for you". Marriage took place on 29th May 1849. At the time of marriage, Pasteur was busy with an experiment and people were worried about his where about. When he was traced in laboratory and asked about his wedding he calmly answered "I was finishing my work". This couple had mutual understanding and led a life of fame but suffered the jealous hatred of fellow scientists and traditionalists in the early days.

Pasteur entered the biological field and framed an opinion about the most controversial issue namely 'Origin of Life'. Tradition was firmly and positively on the side that life can originate spontaneously out of dead matter. Pasteur carried out series of experiments to prove that life originates from life. He was vehemently criticized for this. Pasteur explained to his wife—"A man of science should think of what will be said of him in the coming centuries, not of the insults or the compliments of the present day" There was a commission to judge the reality about origin of life which passed the decision in favour of Pasteur. Pasteur then tried experiments and kept thinking in the direction of preservation of life.

In France, mysterious disease had attacked the silkworms in the province of Alias and silk industry was in danger (1860). Pasteur received an urgent message to investigate it. Pasteur was completely unaware of the field but his patient working and scientific approach could result in success. During those days he lost three of his children but Pasteur remained unperturbed and duty bound. During these days he also suffered a mild paralytic attack (1868). Irrespective of this he kept on working. Such was his sacrifice for his country.

Pasteur's conclusion about silkworm epidemic was diseased eggs. The silkworm seed merchants were responsible for this as they sold "bad seed for good money". These merchants were annoyed and troubled Pasteur to the maximum extent. Pasteur, working 18 hours a day with a microscope resolved the problem of pathology (1865-70). Disease was due to particular bacterium. He could trace bacilli of two distinct diseases. Pasteur could thus solve the problem of agriculture and people of Alias set up a statue in his honour. Cultivators tried his remedy and produced healthy crops. He would have earned a lot by his research applications but his answer to such queries was "In France, a scientist would be lowering himself if he worked for personal profits"

Another area of his work was fermentation, micro organisms and bacteria in chemical transformations. He proved that micro organisms and bacteria were already present in air and were not generated in decay processes. He carried series of controlled experiments with clear air and at high altitudes of Alps to prove it. Wine, beer, whisky and other liquors were produced in France. It was one of the major industries in the country. There was a problem of 'souring'. Pasteur found out that it was due to bacteria which multiplied at great rate and many were difficult to destroy. Fermentation process without souring was developed by his genius. He should be more remembered not for fermentation but for fermentation of ideas he initiated!

Another technique which is well known now as 'Pasteurization' also was initiated for the purpose. It involves heating the liquid or solution to high temperature (50-70°C) for some time (few seconds or few minutes) and then rapidly cooling. The technique is applied universally to varieties of perishable foods and drinks especially to cream, wine and milk. The taste of food is maintained with elimination of bacteria (poison). He was involved in this work from 1857-67. 'Pasteurization' is now extended up to 'sterilization' especially for inanimate objects to make them free from contaminated micro-organisms and infecting agents. Sterilization involves heating for some time at high temperature = 100°C or more. This quick Pasteurization is called 'Flash Pasteurisation'.

Pasteur was then interested in by arresting diseases in animals and human beings, detailed study of micro organisms, germs and bacteria. In post-war period he tried to put his ideas to improve results of surgery. Death rates after surgical operations were appalling. The maternity hospitals were referred to as ante-chambers of death. Surgeons kept on killing patients with old fashioned methods. Pasteur studied the problem and concluded that all massacre was due to contamination of wounds, instruments, hands of surgeon, sponges, bandages, utensils etc. during operation by germs, bacteria and various microbes. That resulted into infections and cause of numerous disease and disorders. He was ridiculed by the surgeons and he researched in the medical field. However, Professor Joseph Lister from the University of Edinburgh (Scotland) took hint from Pasteur's advice. He disinfected all things related to his surgical operations by carbolic acid. As a result fatalities of his surgical cases drastically reduced from ninety per cent to fifteen per cent. It was still very difficult to get roots to Pasteur's idea in medical field as "It was a new (novel) idea and therefore it was a bad idea" was the psyche of the people. One of the physicians Dr. Guerin was violent on Pasteur's ideas and even challenged Pasteur to a dual Pasteur calmly reacted... "My business is to heal, not to kill".

"Preservation of Life" is the most important contribution by Pasteur. It originated in his simple method of transforming a virus into a vaccine. It saved innumerable lives. His methodical research led to an important discovery immunizing the person (living being) against deadly disease by inoculating the being with a mild and very dilute form of that disease. The fight back survival mechanism in living body is kept alert and efficient due to this.

He applied it to epidemic of anthrax. The sheep and cattle industry of France was in danger due to anthrax—a deadly fever of spleen. His methods proved to be boon to cattle industry. He could prepare vaccine to save fowl from chicken cholera. He could control rabies among dongs and hydrophobia among those bitten by a mad dog. He had a courage to experiment with such odd situations and try to overcome the resistance from medical people. He put his life to extreme danger nearing death when he sucked saliva from the mouth of mad enraged dog for the purpose. He inoculated the anti rabies principle in human being. The dramatic example was a nine year old boy Joseph Meister bitten by a mad dog. Pasteur took the risk and saved the life. The boy was completely cured and Pasteur conquered hydrophobia.

Such was Pasteur's need based achievements to extend the frontiers of life. He however remained modest religious and patient all the time in spite of overwhelming popularity and also during earlier disgraces. In his honour

'Pasteur Institute' was established. The France government released currency note for Five Francs with his photograph and pictorial presentation of his research work like fermentation, sheep, fowls, dog, silk worms, vaccine etc. His seventieth birthday was celebrated nationwide and function was arranged at Sorbonne.

As he said, he devoted his life for research only. He had only one hobby, i.e. drawing. He used to prepare nice sketches and paintings of his parents and forefathers. His nice sketch is carved and cast for ever, in healthy advancement of human race even after his death on 27th September 1895. May his soul rest in peace!

7

Alfred Nobel

There can be greater contradiction than that summed up in the life of Alfred Nobel. Nobel yearned for world peace and became multimillionaire by selling merchandise of death to all who would pay its price. His business was inherited from his father and there was no logic to it. Though, in later years, Nobel had tried to give some points. Nobel did not invent and propagate 'Dynamite' for peaceful purposes or benefit of mankind nor did he so to destruct and destroy. His simple reasons were—business, its prosperity through innovativeness and inventions, withstand the competitions with quality and patents (business creates) and ultimately profit motive. Utilization of wealth gained thus could be different point. Explosives are being used in many places for betterment of mankind. It is indeed one of the important branches of applied chemistry. They are used in mining industry, rail, road and building programmers

and quarrying. Their proper use can certainly be beneficial for mankind. However, two world wars became the demonstrations of their harmful applications and horrible results. It is so with anything to greater or lesser extent. Many medicines in small quantities and property, used serve as elixirs of life but in large quantities and improperly used can be poisonous and deadly. The thinking of such type can give some consolation to Nobel's contradictory life and his saying "Inventing a weapon with such horrible capacity for mass annihilation would make wars impossible." In reality however, a weapon even like atom bomb had been used and mankind is facing the consequences still. Such contradictions do exist in every field, however contradiction in case of Nobel is ever glorified due to Nobel Prizes in five important disciplines of knowledge—Physics, Chemistry—Physiology or medicine, Literature and more so in Peace since 1901. The sixth Nobel Prize is given for Economics since 1969.

Alfred Nobel was small in stature, insignificant looking, self effacing and suffered chronic illness throughout his life. He however, kept him busy and upright in research activity and business all the way. He was cynical and pessimistic on one hand while idealistic and benevolent on the other. He was pacifist and a lover of poetry. He preferred his own company. He never married. He was a brilliant conversationalist. He used to talk intelligently with men and gallantly with women. He distrusted everybody's motive. He tried to write poems and during last phase of life he tried to write drama. These attempts were proved to be pathetic. He was inventor of dynamite and many other high explosives. Money was cascading on him for ten years from his mighty international munitions business. He earnestly desired that wealth should be used for the purpose of promoting friendship between nations and bringing about whole or partial disarmament. He was also promoter of research activities of dreamers and idealists. Today his reputation rests, not on his inventive genius but on the international Nobel Awards.

He was born on 21st October, 1833 at Stockholm. His forefathers were peasants but his father, Immanuel, was military engineer. Alfred inherited talent, application orientation and engineering (technological) approach from his father.

His mother came from Swedish naturalist family. His father had to face bankruptcy in the year in which Alfred was born. He left for Finland in search of new career and joined the family back after four years. During these days his mother brought him up with his two brothers. Strong bond was woven between him and his mother which remained unbroken for the rest of Alfred's life. He had strong emotional and affectionate involvement with his mother. It is said to be one of the reason of his being unmarried. During his childhood he was quite sickly and weak, He owed his survival to his mother's devoted nursing and ceaseless care.

Immanuel then concentrated on explosives business. Czar of Russia was interested in this business and Nobel family shifted to St. Petersburg (1842) then capital of Russia. It is Leningrad today. The family was provided with lavish amenities and all the comforts of life. The children were brought up by engaging Swedish tutor. Alfred was able to learn then five languages—Russian, English, French, German and of course Swedish. Immanuel prospered in Russia. His explosive mines were success and his talents poured out inventions which he marketed with profit. He received Imperial Gold medal from Czar at court. When Alfred was sixteen, he was sent abroad to have a look at the world and to get work and live experiences. He travelled in Europe (many countries) and to America, New York. In America he was placed with John Ericson—Mechanical Engineer. Ericson was architect of ironclad warship 'Monitor'. Alfred's interests remained with Chemistry of explosive and inventions of new explosives and he joined back to father's business. However, he could get an idea about world wide market for his future business. The Crimean war of 1854 ended with disaster in Nobel's factory. There was fire in the factory and second bankruptcy had to be faced.

Alfred studied new liquid-nitroglycerine discovered in 1847 by an Italian chemist—Ascanio Sobrero. Alfred came back to Stockholm with his parents and kept on experimenting with nitroglycerine. On 14th October 1863, Alfred Nobel was granted his patent for his nitroglycerine product. Idea that was crystallizing in his mind following years was—using a small amount of one explosive to produce the shock which would blow up a large volume of another explosive—would be great step ahead in high explosive field. The principle is known as primary charge. Alfred worked with this idea along with his brother Oscar Emil who was a student at Stockholm University. An explosion wrecked his laboratory (1864) and killed four people including his brother Oscar Emil. Alfred was distraught but he felt, it was a dangerous occupation and who worked in it must risk their lives. Immanuel was shocked and lost interests in explosive. His inventive mind was then focussed on wood shavings and saw dust and their gluing together to get plywood. His father died in 1872.

Nobel continued with his business. He hired a barge and anchored it on a lake two miles away from Stockholm and carried his production and experiments in the barge. Nitroglycerine was potential danger in transport, careless handling, factory and due to leakage. It caused sensation after sensation in Europe. Nobel changed its name and marketed under friendly sounding name—'glonion oil'. Alfred has the fear of widespread panic by repeated accident in nitroglycerine factories, that would result in ban on the manufacture of nitroglycerine.

Dynamite was discovered by Nobel by chance. Nitroglycerine that leaked could be absorbed by the clay prevalent in northern Germany called Kiesel guhr. It has large capacity to absorb and could still remain granular and could react with heat and shock as did nitro-glycerin. He detonated it with percussion cap and found that it worked better than the oil. It was also called 'Nobel's safety powder'. In 1867 Nobel and Co. started shipping dynamite in huge quantities. In 1868, Alfred Nobel received Gold Medal from Swedish Academy of Science for "Outstanding, original work in the realm of art, literature and science or for important discoveries of practical value for mankind". This had satisfactory effect on Nobel though he had general contempt for honours and awards.

His factories mushroomed all over Europe and America. He found American business not to his likings and left it since 1885. It was then left to DuPont Empire which became giant company in many fields later on. France refused nitro-glycerine but Nobel made his residence at Paris—San Remo. It was lavish, kingly place to live in. He passed most of his time there. He established at Ardeer (Britain) the greatest dynamite factory in the world. Nobel tried to absorb nitro-glycerine on powdered charcoal, brick dust or even cement and gave way to many explosive formulations. He also used fulminate of mercury for detonation [$Hg(ONC)_2$]

There is one interesting story about discovery of another explosive 'Blasting Gelatine' Nobel had a finger cut. He put up a film of collodion-nitrated cotton to heal it. It could not work and he was kept awake due to pains and was set thinking about other explosive. The idea struck to his mind and he prepared jelly like mass by mixing collodion and nitro-glycerine. It was 'Blasting Gelatine' used as controlled propellant for military use.

He further discovered 'ballistite' in 1888 which was commonly called 'smokeless powder'. There was court matter with British Government about formulation of explosive 'Cordite' whose formula according to Nobel was that of 'ballistite'. He however lost the suit. This indicated his fighting nature for research and business. He also designed other dynamites like 'straight dynamite' which consisted dynamite, sodium nitrate and organic fuels. Sodium nitrate served as source of oxygen. Similarly, ammonium dynamite was prepared by replacing sodium nitrate with ammonium nitrate. Ammonium dynamite was less sensitive to flame and shock. Alfred has huge number of patents (355) at his credit.

Now explosive industry has added many powerful names. Some of them are TNB (trinitrobenzene), TNT (Trinitrotoluene), RDX (cyclonite) and PETN (pentaerythritol tetranitrate). They have produced sensations by terrorists and extremists. They can also be used efficiently for betterment of mankind.

Though Nobel was lonely throughout his life it is worth noting two of his associations. One was with remarkable woman – Bertha Von Suttner. They had platonic association. She was his secretary, in Paris. She spoke four languages and had the beauty and poise of perfect lady. Her wit, intelligence and integrity captivated Nobel. Bertha married in Austria with Arthur Bertha became famous throughout Western Europe as the nineteenth century's most inspired propagandist for peace. Her greatest inspiration was: The Nobel Peace Prize.

Bertha wrote a Novel which swept Europe. It was "Lay down Arms!" It was written in German. Bertha had long discussions and arguments with Nobel and letter written by Nobel to her on 7th January 1893 had first reference about Peace Prize. She got 1905's Nobel Peace Prize.

Other association was with Sophie Hess, a Viennese shop girl which lasted from 1876 for eight years. This affair was noticed quite late in 1950 when the Nobel Institute in Stockholm disclosed the existence of 216 letters written to her by Alfred. It appeared that the lady had no integrity and her association with Alfred was not deep rooted. These are just casual references.

The Nobel Prize fund was of 9 million dollars. The Prize consists of gold medal, citation (diploma) and cash prize. Cash prize varies from time to time. It was 1,20,000 dollars in 1973. Peace prize is given at Oslo by King or Queen of Norway and other prizes are given at Stockholm by King or Queen of Sweden. The Prize distribution ceremony takes place on 10th December on the death anniversary. Nobel died on 10th December 1896. The work of selection of names for the prizes is carried with utmost care. It is reflected by the fact of very high esteem and recognition to the great Nobel Prizes. Royal Swedish Academy of sciences selects the names for awards in Physics, Chemistry and Economics. Caroline Institute of Stockholm selects names for awards in physiology or medicine. Swedish Academy selects the names for awards in literature. The experts are also involved in the process. The committee of five persons chosen by Norwegian Parliament selects the names for awards in peace. One can't recommend his own name but other individuals or institutes can do it for him. The first peace award was divided between Henri Dunant of Switzerland (the founder of the Red Cross) and Frederic Passy, a veteran French pacifist though Nobel had clearly wished to have it for Bertha Von Suttner. This clearly indicated objectivity, universal acceptability and greatness of Nobel Prizes. Utmost care is taken to avoid completely subjectivity, personal influences and politics while selecting the names for Nobel Prizes. Such is the fascination account of Nobel's life whose shining genius remained cloud clad due to glorious international awards which bear his name.

8

Madame Marie Curie

It is probably the most unique example in scientific explorations that two generations, over sixty years worked in the similar fields. It is the Curie family. Not only that but it is also exceptional case that woman scientist—Marie got two times Nobel Prize, one in 1903 shared with Pierre Curie and Henry Becquerel for Physics and the other in 1911 for Marie Curie alone for chemistry. To add further, in 1935 Marie's daughter Irene Curie with her husband Fredric Joliot got Nobel Prize for synthesis of new radioactive elements. Marie Curie was the most modest celebrated woman. Albert Einstein remarked about her as "Marie Curie is among all distinguished people, the only one whom fame has not corrupted." Curie family worked over a wide range from crystal symmetry to modern nuclear physics. The atom which was thought to be indivisible further was shown to consist of different subatomic particles. Radioactivity, nuclear fission and nuclear reactions, radioisotopes, artificial radioactivity, magnetic properties, Pyro and Piezo electricity etc are the major areas of research covered by this

unique family. Still more characteristic feature of this family was their strong nationalistic and human approach. Pierre Curie in his talk while receiving Nobel Prize in 1903 warned about 'radioactivity' in criminal hands as the bane to human race. Marie Curie with daughter Irene visited many soldier camps for medical diagnosis and cure. They remained at most conscious about not disclosing the source of radioactive elements and detailed information of their potential in preparing nuclear bomb to Nazis. During war struck period they tried to conceal their research and lived in Paris endangered of their lives for the sake of protection of human race. They got great fame and name but the scientific research was not used for their personal benefits. The money created and generated out of their research was put further for the cause of scientific pursuits only. Their needs were very less and their luxuries were ordinary and simple form of relaxations—small cycle trips or so. Irene and Frederic also campaigned for the peaceful and positive role of their research and tried to prevent the psyche of the people and especially administrators from the devastating and far reaching effects of nuclear weapons even for the sake of scientific trials. France remained on the forefront of nuclear research because of the Curie family. The first nuclear reactor Zoë was installed in 1948 under General De Gaulle's leadership in France. Everybody's life study from Curie family is motivating and unending source of inspiration. They were distinguished individual personalities by themselves but still interlinked by common strong threads of scientific achievements and human well beings. Old saint '*Dadhichi*' sacrificed his body and offered it to '*Indra*' (God) for human protection. Similar is the story of these modern '*Dadhichis*'. Amongst them Marie Curie remained the lone.... star. Marie Curie was the first known victim of radioactivity. She was personification of Goddess of Knowledge '*Saraswati*' and '*Kohinoor*' diamond amongst the great scientists.

Manya Sklodowska (Marie Curie) was born in Warsaw (Poland) on 7th November 1867. Her forefathers were nobel and honest peasants. Her parents however had risen above the soil into the atmosphere of higher education. Her father was a teacher of physics at the Warsaw high school and her mother was an accomplished pianist. She inherited her father's brain and mother's hands.

She showed an early aptitude for experimental science and voracious reading. She was extra ordinarily brilliant. She could easily remember the lessons that her elder sister wanted to remember, incidentally and correct her. She was the youngest of the five children. She lost her eldest sister and mother at very early stage of life. It was then sad impoverished family.

Marie's father was involved in the freedom movement of Poland from the tyranny of Russian Czar. He had therefore lost his position in the high school. Against this feeble background Marie had to live and progress. It was the great struggle for achievements—to survive and prosper mentally and physically. She was rebel from the beginning; she had the polish heart with aspirations of free country. She had fighting spirit against adversity and tyranny. She loved her country beyond anything and had keen interest in the history of Poland. She had to toil against poverty and for education. She was very untidy in her appearance but was beautiful. She had many skills and arts. Her hobbies included roaming in the woods, swinging, swimming, fishing, sewing and crafts work. She was exceptionally good and graceful dancer. She was quite responsive. In her school days Russian language study was compulsory. It was the point of her hatred. Once in school her teacher, Anthonia Tupakka, was narrating the story of polish king Augustus. The king was great with many good and noble qualities but he was weak minded. During the lesson Czar dominated inspector rushed in the class and asked about the activities going on. Manya could answer the questions so intelligently and shrewdly that the inspector couldn't even smell of the conspiracy that was going on in the class. She completed her school course in 1883 and carried off the Gold Medal. This was the first indication of turning Gold Princess of school days into Radium Queen Nobel laureate in future.

Marie's older sister Bronya wanted to study at Sorbonne in Paris for medical degree. Marie decided to earn for her sister's education by working as governess – teaching servant. During this job her first love affair took place with one named Casmir, but in vain. It was strong blow at the dreaming age. She felt like to suicide but overcome the feeling and started working patiently to earn for Bronya.

Marie then joined University of Sorbonne at the age of 23 in the faculty of science. She was attentive student on the first row at lectures. She was however introvert and lonely. The boys used to remark about her – 'fine hair, fine eyes, fine figure of a girl but the trouble is, she won't talk to anybody'. She led the life of monk for four years. In a small room with no heat and no water, she lived on a general diet of bread, butter and tea. Rarely, she could have luxury of an egg or a fruit. She lived in the world of her books, experiments and lecturers. Her intellectual domain encompassed physics, chemistry, mathematics, poetry, music, astronomy and what not. She took her masters degree in physics (1893) and that in mathematics (1894).

At Paris she came in contact with Pierre Curie. He was the son of French Physician with brilliant career. He was first rank scientist Marie and Pierre matched each other perfectly—they were the travellers to the exclusive pursuit of science. Pierre found in Marie beloved friend, faithful wife, intelligent and inquisitive student and great researcher. He had formulated the principle of symmetry in the structure of crystals. He had found our phenomena of Pyro-electricity—generation of electricity due to heat and Piezo-electricity—generation of electricity on other axis due to pressure on one of the axis of non-conducting crystals like quartz. He devised analytical and torsion balances. He studied magnetic properties at different temperatures and their transitions from ferromagnetism to para magnetism to dia magnetism, Ferro magnetic substances acquire and maintain magnetism *e.g.* iron. Diamagnetic substances are repelled by magnetic field and paramagnetic substances acquire magnetic properties to very small extent. The symmetry principle in crystals was extended further in symmetry principles of human behaviour as a result. Marie and Pierre got married in 1895. The marriage was partnership of genius and comradeship of love. Marie gave birth to two girl children. Irene who carried further the title of Marie was born on 12th September 1897.

Later on, this scientist couple took interest in the experiments of Henri Becquerel. Becquerel was working with 'rare metal—Uranium' salts. He found that these salts emitted rays which could penetrate opaque objects. He had placed photographic plate wrapped by black paper near uranium salts. He noticed that photographic plate could get some impressions even through it was wrapped. These strange rays led to discovery of radioactivity (1896). Radioactivity was the name coined by Marie—the spontaneous emergence and penetrating property of certain types of rays from certain substances.

Madame Curie took keen interest in this work. She went through long, arduous and heart breaking road. Though the laboratory in which they were working was old fashioned shed and the apparatus were pitiably inadequate, they concluded that property of uranium salts was atomic/nuclear. This was the principle that led to invention of atomic bomb (1945) Curie thought that Uranium salts were not only substances that could emit rays but there could be other too! She submitted many substances for rigorous tests and found that the element thorium had similar power of same degree. She further noticed still powerful source of radioactivity in some minerals and thought it to be due to a new elements. She studied for the purpose the ore, called Pitchblende—an oxide of Uranium. Pitchblende from which isolation of suspected new element was to be carried out was an expensive ore. Pitchblende was mined in Bohemian, a part of Austria. Bohemia was famous for the manufacture of glass—crystal glass. Pitchblende that remained after extraction of Uranium was worthless. They got it at meagre cost of transportation. The couple worked for four years with pitchblende—shovelling, gasping and coughing at the noxious fumes. They did not bother anything except to get new elements. Fortunately, they could get not one new element but two, one was named Polonium after Marie's native country and other was named Radium. Marie, as made clear earlier was strong nationalist. She was interested to settle in Poland. Pierre was also ready to settle in Poland for her sake. But more universal science prevailed over narrow national outlook and for the reason they settled in Paris and could discover Polonium (1898). It reflected their views about both- science and nation! Radium was then isolated in 1902 and its atomic weight was determined to be 225. The therapeutic (medicinal) value of radium was soon established. It was found effective on many treatments, even on cancer. People insisted on them to get the process of extraction of radium patented. They however refused to do so for their personal benefits. Their views were—"Radium is the instrument of mercy and it belonged to the world". Such was the broad universal outlook. Even when she received 1 gm of Radium from the fund raised by American Women (1921), she had the same opinion.

Curie's got many honours and awards. They however were interested to set the laboratory for research. They remained aloof from the same. Marie was simple in living. She used to wear usually untidy black dress presenting her as a peasant woman. One day an American reporter visited their cottage in Le Pouldu where they were on vacation for fishing. He mistook Marie as the house keeper and Marie also pretended so. The message that was given by her to the reporter was interesting – "Be less inquisitive about people and more inquisitive about ideas." Soon they got good laboratory and Pierre was appointed as the professor at Sorbonne.

There was one great calamity on Marie's life. The accidental death of her husband took place in April 1906. Marie's happiness was at end but her work took still powerful wings. She was to fulfil the dreams of her husband. She assumed the professorship at Sorbonne in place of Pierre. It was the first occasion that woman was appointed to such high position. She worked hard to keep her busy and to eliminate the thoughts of Pierre which were too intense. She was to survive for children's sake and "for science and humanity" sake. Marie's first lecture as a professor arose, lot of curiosity amongst the scientific world. Usually polish people were taken as inferior genius and moreover Marie was a woman. Her lecture got loud applause. She presented her views with twinkle of brilliance in her eyes, calmly, logically and with confidence. She won the minds of her admirers and critics too. Marie was an excellent teacher. She modified science teaching effectively based on experimental demonstration.

The last quest of her life was to unravel healing power of radium and other radiations and radioisotopes. Radioisotopes are the atoms of the same element with different atomic weights. Atoms have fixed atomic number but they can differ in atomic weights. Some of them are: C-14, I-128, Co-60, P-35, Fe-55 etc.

During World War—I Marie organized and supervised X-ray stations and X-ray care for the wounded. She trained hundred of people working on Roentgen X-ray machines. Thousands of wounded passed through her hands. She travelled throughout the length and breadth of the country caring for wounded. She was an angel of mercy with a beautiful face and tired and acid-bitten long fingers. In her mission Irene Curie took active part. At the end of the war she had the double satisfaction of peace and free Poland. Her native land, slave for a century and a half become free and jubilant again.

At Warsaw in 1932 Maria Sklodowska—Curie Radium Institute was established. She was offered Director's position, she declined to accept it. She however provided every kind of help human and material resources for the institute. Her work was thus well recognized and appreciated by the fellow countrymen and the world.

Madame Curie travelled the unconventional way throughout her life. She faced many stumbling blocks to her road but she kept on continuously till she died a martyr to her work on 4th July 1934.

9

Friedrich Wöhler

The term 'organic' was used conveniently to designate substances derived from plant or animal sources or the degraded products of these sources. A few of substances were known since earliest antiquity, prehistoric peoples were knowing sugar, its fermentation product wine which contains ethyl alcohol, vinegar (dilute solution of acetic acid) produced during souring of wine and alike. Vegetable oils and animal fats and the process of making soap from these substances have been known for centuries. Methods of applying the beautiful vegetable dye indigo and of dyeing with madder root (alizarin) were developed by ancient Romans and Egyptians. There were the chief dyes for fabrics. Tyrian purple was the dye extracted from a rare species of mollusk. The middle ages only added few organic substances. During the 16th and 17th centuries some advances resulted from pyrolysis of plant products. Dry distillation of wood afforded crude mixture of methyl alcohol, acetone and acetic acid (now known) called pyro ligneous acid. These organic compounds contain relatively few elements namely carbon hydrogen, oxygen and nitrogen etc. In

sharp contrast, the substances from mineral origin were referred to 'inorganic'. Here diversification in elemental composition proved to be the rule. In 1807 thirty six elements were known and by 1830 this list reached fifty three. Berzelius undertook the study of organic compounds and thought that organic compounds could arise through operation of 'Vital Force' inherent in living cell. He further held that the chemical synthesis of organic substances was beyond the realm of possibility.

The doctrine of an essential vital force remained unchallenged until Wöhler was led through a chance observation reported in 1828, to the discovery that organic compounds can arise without the agency of any organism. Wöhler obtained urea (organic compound present in human urine) by evaporating aqueous (water) solution of inorganic salt ammonium cyanate.

$$\underset{\text{Ammonium Cyanate}}{NH_4OCN} \xrightarrow{\text{Heat}} \underset{\text{Urea}}{CO(NH_2)_2}$$

Note that in above two compounds there is 1 Carbon 4 Hydrogen 1 oxygen and 2 nitrogen atoms. There is only structural change in arrangement of atoms in a molecule. The result was so contrary to the thought of the period and startling that Wöhler repeated the experiment many times before publication of his results. Wöhler when fully convinced about his reports wrote to Berzelius 'I must tell you that I can prepare urea without requiring a kidney or animal, either man or dog'. The discovery eventually led to abandonment of the idea of a vital force. Some people even retreated to new lines of defence, arguing that urea was only an excretory substance—a product of breakdown and not of synthesis. During following years many organic compounds were synthesized even from elements and Wöhler got the recognition as 'The Father of Organic Chemistry', chemical historian Thorpe wrote—'That should be accounted a red letter day in the history of science. By demonstrating that urea can be made synthetically by ordinary laboratory processes and from substances inorganic in their origin, Wöhler proved that vital force is only another name for chemical action, and that animal is nothing but a laboratory in which multitude of chemical changes, similar to those which occur in our test tubes.. is continually taking place' Thorpe has little bit exaggeration but fact remains.

In 1935, Wöhler wrote to Berzelius 'Organic' chemistry just now is enough to drive one mad. It gives me the impression of a primeval tropical forest, full of the most remarkable things—a monstrous and boundless thicket, with no way to escape, into which one may well dread to enter' Such is the vast scope of organic chemistry.

The designation organic has persisted as a convenient and reasonably descriptive classification of a group of chemical compounds having many common characteristics. Organic chemistry however is now defined as the chemistry of carbon compounds. They contain carbon, hydrogen, oxygen, nitrogen, halogen, sulfur, phosphorous, some metals and very few other elements. These compounds are enormously large in number and it goes on increasing at very high rate. All other compounds of rest elements taken together is quite small in number as compared to organic compounds. This is mainly because of unique property of carbon element to combine with itself to form rings, chains (straight or branched) *i.e.* Catenation. Secondly, valency of carbon is 4 so it can have large permutations and combinations with other elements *i.e.* it can combine with 4 hydrogen, 2 hydrogen,1 oxygen, 2 hydrogen, 2 chlorines or 1 hydrogen and 3 chlorines etc. This valency 4 is of covalent type sharing of electrons between two atoms. Thirdly there is isomerism—compounds having same molecular formula but different structural formulae observed to a large extent. These isomerism are further of various types. German chemist Angust Kekule has contributed a great deal about the structures of organic compounds and especially the structure of benzene (obtained from coal tar) One can get an idea about the role of isomers in organic compounds by following data. The simplest organic compounds are hydro carbons containing only carbon and hydrogen elements. Hydrocarbon with Formula $C_{10}H_{22}$ can have 75 different structures and so different 75 compounds similarly $C_{20}H_{42}$ formula can have 366,319 structures and hence that many compounds. Common glucose with formula $C_6H_{10}O_6$ have sixteen isomers and as number of elements increase in the formula number of isomers goes on multiplying.

Organic compounds are structurally very sensitive. They transform into other compounds by application of heat, acidic and basic media, and large number of chemical reagents. These compounds, however, encompass all the walks of human life and hence very important. Morrison and Boyd, two professor of New York University, have nicely commented about this field in their quite popular text book of organic chemistry as—"Organic Chemistry is a field of immense importance to technology. It is the chemistry of dyes and drugs, paper and ink, paints and plastics, gasoline and rubber tyres; it is the chemistry of the food we eat and the clothing we wear. It is a field that is fundamental to medicine and biology; aside from water, living organisms are made up chiefly of organic compounds and biological processes are ultimately a matter of organic chemistry" Naturally, the boost for this field by Wöhler's discovery refuting 'Vital Force' is a mile stone in development of the field and hence he is rightly called 'Father of Organic Chemistry'

Wöhler was born on July 1800 at Eschersheim near Frankfurt am Main. He was interested right from earlier days in chemistry and he had a hobby of collecting mineral specimens. He was admitted to Marburg University for medicine studies in 1820. He took the degree in 1823 from Heidelberg in medicine, surgery and obstetrics. Gmelin advised him to concentrate in chemistry. He was influenced by the work of Berzelius. Berzelius was the first scientist to give symbols to elements. He also coined the term 'isomerism'. Berzelius in a sense was a motivator to Wöhler. They however, stood date as fast friends. Wöhler took teaching assignments in Technical Schools in Berlin (1825-1831) and also in Cassel (1831-1836). He was an outstanding teacher and therefore many students used to gather for his lectures. He had more devotion to lectures and less interest for laboratory side. He used to attend each of his students personally. He was kind hearted. Apart from academic progress of the student, he used to take personal interest in their domestic, social and personal lives and problems. He used to actively help and advise them. Along with teaching he did translation of Berzelius's work in the form of books in organic, inorganic and analytical chemistry. As a student himself he was not outstanding student.

Wöhler's discovery 'urea synthesis' was opposed by Liebig also. Liebig was founder of agricultural chemistry. He studied soil fertilization by synthetic chemical fertilizers. Wöhler got married in 1829 to his cousin Franziska. He could have one son and unfortunately in 1832 his wife died in giving birth to a daughter. He was then quite disturbed and lonely, He undertook research with Liebig as a solace. They studied oil of bitter almonds and could isolate its important constituent benzaldehyde. While studying the properties of benzaldehyde they noticed that part of the structure participates in chemical reactions as an entity (later it came out to be functional group in general). In benzaldehyde they studied 'benzyl part' that moves as a unit. They also studied sodium benzoate an important food preservative, quinine which is used for tanning leather, hydroquinone used as photographic developer and antiseptic (It is also used for combating fever). Inorganic compounds are studied based on the position of elements (their electronic configuration) in them in a periodic table. Elements and their compounds show similar trends in their properties for example metal sodium (Na) and potassium (K) and their carbonates Na_2CO_3 and K_2CO_3. In case of organic compounds this similarity trend is seen due to the functional groups like say alcohol, aldehyde, acid, halide etc. Organic chemistry therefore is many times referred as chemistry of 'Functional Groups'.

Wöhler got married in 1834 for second time with his first wife's friend Julie Pfeiffer. She had two daughters.

Wöhler was able to isolate pinhead particles of Aluminium (Al) in 1845. He studied its properties like specific gravity, ductility, colour and stability in air. It has become now one of the important metals because of its lightness and durability. He also studied its alloys with magnesium. The reaction that was used for the purpose was $3\ K + AlCl_3 \rightarrow Al + 3KCl$.

The name that is associated with isolation of aluminium is of Charles Martin Hall. He was able to obtain it from Bauxite by cheaper method. Wöhler was able to isolate another metal Beryllium (Be) by similar chemical reaction. Beryllium is used for fluorescent lighting. It however has not hardness and rigidity. It is poisonous and dangerous to handle.

Wöhler discovered in 1862 one of the most important compound of calcium namely calcium carbide—CaC_2. This compound reacts with water and acetylene gas is obtained. This gas is used in oxyacetylene flames which are used as blow torch solders. Acetylene is one of the important organic compounds and used as a starting material for many polymers like neoprene (first synthetic rubber, made in America), polyvinyl chloride (PVC) and alike. From acetylene many other organic compounds are also produced.

Wöhler also studied chemical relationship between 'C' Carbon and 'Si' Silicon. So also with Titanium—Ti. Carbon and silicon are non-metals and Titanium is metallic in character. He studied the reaction between Titanium tetrachloride and ammonium hydroxide. This resulted in smoky/ foggy material. It is referred as smoke screen and used for sky writing by aviators. He had contributed to large scale manufacture of nickel and extension of silicon chemistry. Unique property of catenation observed in Carbon which is combined with itself to form rings and chains, is also observed to some extent in silicon. He also discovered amygdalin in 1837. It is present in bitter almonds. Now it is proved that its structure consists of three parts namely benzaldehyde, glucose and hydrocyanic acid.

In 1824, during the Wöhler work with cyanogen and aqueous ammonia i.e. ammonium cyanate, other compound oxalic acid was also obtained. In fact oxalic acid is also organic compound but less was talked about oxalic acid and mostly it was area that was in focus. It was also in the same year that Berzelius 'isomerism' concept was substantiated by Wöhler Examples were silver cyanate AgNCo and silver fulminate AgONC. The properties of these two compounds are altogether different. Silver fulminate is highly explosive where as silver cyanate is not. One is Silver salt of fulminic acid (HONC). Note that inorganic compounds rarely witness 'isomerism'. Above two silver salts and two acids are however, isomers.

Wöhler was appointed as Professor of Chemistry at Gottingen in 1836. He also became the Chairman of Chemistry on the medical faculty of Gottingen. He died on 23rd September 1882 at the same place. Most of his life's work was carried on at this place. His statue is erected in the campus of Gottingen. He was highly respected.

Wöhler was the person who got the degree in medicine but worked on the field of chemistry. Similar is the case of Sir Alexander Fleming who gets the degree in medicine but carried the research in bacteriology. Whereas the case of Louis Pasteur is otherwise, he got the degree in chemistry but except his earlier work on crystallizations most of his work was related to living organisms and biology/medicine. Wöhler's discovery of urea from ammonium cyanate, and Fleming's discovery of penicillin and lysozyme are both chance of accidental discoveries. These discoveries however are proved to be the important turning points in the history of development of science. In this context one should remember the sentence of Pasteur—'In the field of experimentation chance favours the prepared mind'. Vivid example of this is the story of Alexander Fleming—Penicillin and Lysozyme. Example of Wöhler is also not less vivid. Wöhler with perseverance, an analytical mind, imagination, curiosity and determination had got the recognition as 'Father of Chemistry'. He was simple, unselfish, loyal, modest and quite normal in his behaviour. Therefore, his contemporary workers who were equally responsible to lay the foundations of organic chemistry would have also liked to call him so.

10

Albert Einstein

Albert Einstein is the greatest man of science. He was the most creative intellects in human history. He had passionate sense of social justice and social responsibility. His belief was—'God is subtle but he is not malicious' as indicated in German proverb. He was scientist (mathematician), saint and philosopher. He had deep insight in music. Violin was his pet instrument and ever faithful friend. He was fond of sailing boat and smoking pipe. There are many stories about his absent mindedness. He used to wear untraditional, strange dresses and used to live in his own thoughts and creations. He was a solitary student 'a singular, taciturn, lonely seeker'. He was the most celebrated and talked about man of science. Men of science and common people throughout the world accepted him as a household idol. Fame was the last thing he desired, he had hoped to use his entire life in quiet research. But he had to remark once "Everybody talks about me, and nobody understands me. I have become demigod in spite of myself".

People had gone crazy about him and his

popularity reached to appalling heights. He smiled and said about this—'The public looks upon me as a strange new animal in the circus of the world' He however, remained the most modest of celebrated man.

His ideas brought "Revolution in science—Newtonian ideas overthrown". The 1919 eclipse of sun provided the experiment to test his ideas and they came to be true. Time was the fourth dimension added to the three dimensions of space (length, breadth and height) 'Relativity' and 'Einstein' become inseparable words. The famous Einstein's equation $E = MC^2$ (E = Energy M = Mass and C = velocity of light = 186000 miles per second or 3×10^{10} cm per sec) gave great blow to the earlier concepts. Inter conversion of mass and energy was the epoch making idea of modern atomic age. It was the foundation of atomic energy and also of devastating effect of atom bomb. His research was as remarkable as his character—a strange blend of kindness, intelligence, naivete and novelty. Relativity got such a huge publicity which no other theory even got. As he rightly said about his equation—"Politics are for the moment an equation is for eternity"

He was voracious reader right from the early age. He mastered mathematicians and philosophers like Euclid, Newton, Spinoza and adored poets and musicians like Goethe, Beethoven, Mozart. He found in universe order, harmony and law. Nature was the only truth for him—which was some total of all relative observations. Scientists tried to observe the truth from their own point of view from their own relative position in their own little corner of the vast world. The Universe should be looked upon from every possible other points of view and all views be combined. According to him, it is difficult to understand that man understands the nature. It is a mystery. The most beautiful thing we experience is mysterious. He was the grand old man bringing harmony to the world. His life was harmonious union of science, music thoughts and arts. He was awarded Nobel Prize in 1921. The Prize was given for his work on photoelectric effect and photoelectric cells and not for relativity is worth noting. In his honour one element is named as Einsteinium (Es). Its atomic number is 99 and atomic mass of its most stable isotope is 254.

Einstein was born on 14th March 1879 in the town of Ulm (Germany). The family was then shifted to Munich (1880). His father had started a small electro-chemical factory with his brother. Albert got his interests in scientific and mathematical processes from his uncle; and from his mother, he inherited a deep love of music. His family was Jewish but he was placed in catholic school because of no alternative. He was brought up in both the faiths, therefore. This peculiarity of his upbringing characterized his universal outlook. He was reluctant to become identified with any particular nation, group or faith. Once he had to fill-up the form, there was a column to indicate religion. He wrote under that column 'mosaic'.

He was queer child. He was not enthusiastic, mentally slow and unsociable. His father could not do well with factory and closed it. This family has then shifted to Milan (Italy). Albert was left all alone in Munich. In vacation he visited Milan and found it more suitable to his tastes, His father wanted him to be electrical engineer but Albert remained stubborn in his pursuit to Mathematics. He was then admitted to Zurich Polytechnic Academy (Switzerland 1894-1900). He completed his studies and got teacher's certificate. He deeply studied many subjects especially physics, mathematics, philosophy, music etc. He got the certificate but could not get the job because of he being Jew. Finally, he got a clerical job at the Swiss patent office in Bern (1901). In this office he got lot of time to try and manipulate his observe ideas and calculations. During this period he discussed his work with one of the intimates 'Mileva Mavic' (school mate). They married soon. Einstein had two sons. Later on they divorced. The divorce was agreed with settlement of Nobel Prize money also. This was quite before the award was given, both of them were sure that Einstein would get it, in near future. Einstein married (1919) with one of his distant cousin Elsa (widow from Berlin) His personal life was equally as his childhood. Mileva and Albert had nothing common outside the laboratory. She was earnest, reserved and suspicious slow girl whereas Albert was vague, happy go lucky Bohemian. Elsa could not adjust with the new world of America. She had strong love for Germany and died in 1936. Einstein was born in Germany, he became citizen of Switzerland in

1905. He was migrated to America in 1933 and from 1940 till his death in 1955 (18 April) he was citizen of America. He widely travelled the world. His outlook was thus universal.

When Einstein was 26, in 1905 he published papers on the production and transformation of light and on the electro-dynamics of moving bodies. These papers revolutionized the earlier ideas about time, space, mass, speed, and gravity—totally. He utilized quantum theory to explain photoelectric effect. This led to the invention of photoelectric cell. Energy is not released continuously nor absorbed so but it is released in quantas—packets were the fundamental principle of quantum theory. About light it has dual nature that of particle and that of wave. The light is a photon with both matter/energy sides. These papers led him to University of Zurich. The life there was different from Bern. He had hard time to match with social life with his meagre salary as a junior professor. He had remarked about this later as "In my relativity I set up a clock at every point in space but in reality, I found it difficult to provide even one in my room". In 1911 he was appointed to a better paid professorship in Prague (German University). There was large group of Jews at Prague but Germans looked upon them as inferior citizens. Later on when position was offered in Zurich Polytechnic, he left for Zurich. In 1913 he became Director of Kaiser Wilhelm Physical Institute in Berlin. During this period he professed his Novel ideas to the world and eclipse of the sun in 1919 brought him in lime light.

Contrary to the doctrine of Newton that everything tends naturally to remain at rest, Einstein declared that everything is actually in a state of motion, The velocities of various bodies are relative to one another. For example, two persons sitting in the railway compartment in fast moving train will find themselves stationary with respect to each other but for the person standing on the field outside will find those two persons moving with speed of the train. These velocities keep on changing except one—the velocity of light—186000 miles per second. The law of relativity includes both speed and direction. Suppose we drop a stone from tower to the ground. For us the stone will appear to fall in a straight line. For the theoretical observer or instrument in space, the stone would describe a curved line. For still another observer still different path would be seen. Relative size of the body is also important. All bodies contract in motion. The rate of contraction of moving body increases with its increase speed. A stick measuring a meter in a state of so-called rest would shrink to zero if it were set in motion at the speed of light. Space is relative so also time. Past, present and future are merely three points in time analogues to the three points in space. The star that we see today is the star of million years ago. If the light that comes from it requires million light years to reach earth. If century years ago if any historical event had occurred, we could see it today if a star at a distance of fifty light years reflected it back and we could have that effective mechanism to receive it. Such could be relative interpretation of time, Today upon earth may be yesterday on the other planet and tomorrow on the third planet. Time is a dimension of space and space is a dimension of time. According to Einstein the universe consists of a space—time continuity. None can be expressed independently. These are coordinate aspects of motion in the mathematical approach to reality.

Brownian movement was the observed phenomenon of colloidal particles ultramicroscopic in nature. Some substances form colloidal solutions in solvents like say starch in water. This state is in between true solution (solution of common salt in water) and suspension (muddy water in rainy season). The colloidal particles are in the state of random zigzag motion. They show Tyndall Effect. When light is passed through colloidal solution, the path of light is seen illuminated due to reflections from the surface of particles. Einstein gave mathematical explanation to Brownian movement. [Incidentally, it is worth quoting analogy, as one foreigner had rightly pointed, that our traffic in a city like Calcutta is similar to Brownian movement].

When Europe was exploded on to war (1914), Einstein was very unhappy. He lived in a cosmos of his own ideas. Paper and pencil were his scientific equipments, his mind was the laboratory and thinking was his experiment. Once he was climbing the ladder to change the picture on the wall, he felt down. He started on significant train of thoughts. The fall of the ladder in Einstein's attic played similar role in development of science as the fall of the apple in Newton's garden.

Concept of gravitation was then radically changed. The belief that objects fell as they were pulled down to a centre of gravitation was shaken. There is no 'up' or 'down' in the universe. Einstein said that the motion of body follow the path of least resistance. There are local fields of gravitation. His theory indicates that the shortest distance between two points is not a straight line but a curved line. Gravitation is not the force as Newton has said but curved field in the space time continuum, created by the presence of mass. A ray of light travelling towards the earth from a distant star is deflected when it passed the space around the sun. Einstein calculated mathematically the exact degree of this deflection. This calculation was proved correct at the eclipse of 1919. Two observatories of Cambridge and Greenwich independently verified the Einstein calculations with their observations.

Such are the glimpses of unfathomable ideas and convictions of giant of science. More fascinating and varied point was his most human approach. He lived with the dispassion of a scientist and the compassion of a saint.

Einstein had predicted new state (fifth) of matter as early as in 1925. Bose-Einstein condensate (Matter has solid, Liquid, gas and plasma states—already these four are known) Recent reports in June 1995 are in support of this. Mr. Wieman and Mr. Cornell from university of Colorado are successful in preparing 'super atom' by using six beams of lasers and thereby an exotic evaporation. The rubidium gas was used for the purpose and temperature was reduced to just near absolute zero (-273 °C) . The atomic motion becomes zero or atoms in the state are stand still. This is the new state produced as anticipated by Albert Einstein. This will lead to development of atomic clocks or atom deposition. These clocks will be able to measure millionth of the second or so. Such was the genius of the great man and as time passes one would realize it better and better.

He hated wealth and fame. He was absolutely convinced that no wealth in the world could help humanity further. When First World War was over, he tried to establish his dream of world peace. He had series of lectures for reconciliation in the enemy countries. It was dangerous affair to speak German in the streets of Paris or to stand on London platform to face the hostility of audience. He demonstrated people the design of an interstellar harmony.

He was tried to be assassinated at the hands of a Russian Noble woman. His name topped the black list of the German right wing assassins and he was refuge in Holland. He found people have lost their sense of proportion. He wrote to Austrian psychiatrist Sigmund Freud—people must have an innate lust for hatred and destruction. He interacted with world-wide thinkers including Rabindranath Tagore. He was on journey to India too and shocked to see millions of men living in slave labour. He could not tolerate such human degradation. Similar was the situation in China. He was offered the presidentship of Israel which he refused on the ground that he was not a politician; he was the seeker of truth and humanity. He was sure of his uncertain fate in the hands of Hitler led Germany. He took appointment in Institute of Advanced Study at Princeton, New Jersey. He was sure to get peace and quietness that he needed for human friendship and cosmic dreams. He advocated world Government for attaining international peace after the destruction of Hiroshima in 1945. He had foresight to write to President Roosevelt a letter (famous) explaining potentialities of atomic energy as a military force. This letter resulted in 'Manhattan Project'

The wandering philosopher—mastered, with his mathematical formulae and violin will serve as eternal search light for harmony, peace and humanity for generations to come.

11

Sir Jagdishchandra Bose

Sir Jagdishchandra Bose is probably unique example of perfect blending of eastern especially Indian culture and western quest for pursuit of exploding knowledge particularly that of science. He had three most important qualities of researcher—scientific observations, experimentation and independent thinking. He had also the courage to express himself confidently and logically. He was consistent in his efforts to solve the problems of science. The fascinating point about his research was to develop indigenous equipments, apparatus and experimental kits at quite low cost and with good efficiency. This requires insight and innovativeness. He could prepare and demonstrate many such things. It is also in tune of national interest of our country with limited resources. His life is an illustration of the fact that intelligence is not monopoly of any particular kind of people or particular country, particular race or religion. His work was the answer to the prevalent thought during his time that any quality work could only be done by European people or British. He had noble combat to out root this belief.

Sacrifice is the great virtue of our country.

Bose's life was full of sacrifices. He believed that knowledge and wisdom is not personal wealth but it had to be used for the benefit and betterment of all mankind. One should not derive the material gains out of exploitation of one's knowledge. The things that accrue by this way should be used for furtherance of knowledge. He was most modest and humble being. He was also a popular teacher. During teaching, he used to demonstrate. His lectures therefore used to be the academic feast. Most of other professors were Englishmen and they had all the way doubts about Bose's performance in a class. Fortunately, he proved to be better than many of them even. He had strong trust that education should not be mere transfer of knowledge but it should be thought provoking and should expand the horizons of knowledge. The process tried then will be joyful and creative.

He used to mix with all types of people. There was no any barrier dependent on caste, creed, race, occupation, rich or poor etc. Many of his childhood friends were fishermen, Shepherds, farmers and even the dacoit. He had curiosity and strong desire to help the poor and downtrodden. He did it all the time. The ideal figure before him was that of '*Karna*' from '*Mahabharata*'. He used to respect the elders, he was strong nationalist. It was just possible for him to join the administrative service and get the British Government job with lavish facilities which he declined. He was also not bookish, amongst his likings include playing *e.g.* cricket, literature, various types of arts, to visit historical and religious places in the country and outside, to have friendship with learned and great people. He was an extraordinary person with good gesture for others and malice for none. Bose was known for his magnanimity. Therefore many people exploited his discoveries for their benefits.

Bose was born at Maimansinha in old Bengal on 30th November, 1858. His father Bhagwan Chandra was working as the deputy magistrate. He was very strict officer and also humane in nature. He was social worker and he actively participated in many welfare activities. He used to take risk and carry out many projects or experiments for benefit of persons. For example one dacoit after completing imprisonment was not having the job; Bhagwan Chandra kept him for household work without any hesitation. He used to look after Jagdish Chandra and could inculcate the spirit of adventure in the young mind. He taught him horse riding. There were two big calamities in the lives of Bengali people one in 1874, there was maleria epidemic and in 1880 there was big draught or famine. Bhagwan Chandra helped the people by his resources and also started one factory to give the jobs for the needy and deserving persons. He was all the time worried about upliftment of people and nation. Jagdishchandra was the only son to his parents and there were five sisters. He was quite curious and inquisitive. The serene and natural rich surroundings in Bengal helped him to come up naturally. There were many questions that were enrooted in his mind in the childhood, he tried to solve them in his future life. His mother was also very soft and kind.

Bhagwan Chandra admitted his only son in Bengali medium school and not in English medium school. That school was also started by him only. Later on, Jagdish Chandra was admitted to Saint Xavier's school at Calcutta. During his days at Calcutta he was residing in hotel. It was English medium school and elderly students were naughty and they used to tease him. Once he became angry and beat them, thereafter they stopped teasing him. He further studied in St. Xavier's College and took B.A. degree. There was one physics professor by name Father Eugene Lafont he was his respectable teacher. Bose was therefore, quite good with physics and experimentation. It was decided that Bose should go to England for further studies. His mother being religious minded was not in much favour of this but finally agreed. She was ready to sell her ornaments also for his further studies.

Bose went to England in 1880 with intention to get medical education. During the course one has to dissect the human body, this was not to the liking of Bose, in fact it was to his great dislike. He decided to change the line and he took admission in Cambridge in Christ Church College to study pure sciences. He was suffering by high temperature or fever. He took medicines but without any effects. Then he started boating in river and could become well. The subjects he learnt were physics, chemistry and botany. Prof. Raleigh of physics casted deep impression on his mind and he also could attract the attention of Prof. Raleigh.

In 1884, he took B.A. of Cambridge University and also B.Sc. of London University. It is rare case of getting two degrees in the same year. His professors wanted him to carry further research but Bose wanted to get the service to support his family. He came back in India and took a job of teacher in Presidency College, Calcutta. His father and mother were happy because their son became teacher—a noble job.

In Presidency College, the most of the staff was English people and they were sceptical about the performance of Bose as a teacher in a college. Bose, however, was quite confident and he had indepth knowledge of the subjects and expertise in communication. He became popular professor. There was step-brother treatment for Indian teachers. They used to get less salary. In protest against this, he did not take his salary for three years. During the period however he worked with full integrity and devotion. Principal and Director of Education were much impressed by this and they paid him full salary of three years and also in future. He completed the debts of his parents.

Durgamohan Das was one of the leading figures in Bengal. He was of progressive thoughts and quite cautious about Women education movement. He had also started a school for girls. His daughter, AblaDevi was studying in Medical College of Madras. He was also close friend of Bhagwan Chandra. Jagdish Chandra and AblaDevi were perfect match to each other and naturally they got married in February 1887. AblaDevi proved to be an ideal wife, she shouldered all the responsibilities of household and allowed Jagdish Chandra to concentrate his study, teaching and research. The couple could get one issue but it could not survive. Thus the couple could not get the satisfaction of having daughter or son. AblaDevi had only one focal point of concentration and that was her husband. She assisted and helped all the while whether in India or abroad. She being learned she could assist him in every field and also did cooking, purchases, maintenance of house etc. She had major contribution in Jagdish Chandra's success. She also took keen interest in the school for girls founded by her father and started skill other activities for women. She expired on 25th April 1951 after 14 years of her husband's death.

Sir J.C. Bose was then settled and he was engrossed in teaching and research. After working hours, he would start his research in laboratory. He used to spend his own money on research. In 1894 itself he was successful in epoch making invention 'wireless telegraphy'. He found that electromagnetic waves can be transmitted without wire. He could demonstrate it in his college by producing electromagnetic wave and receive the same at a distance without wire connections. Recent documentary evidence is in favour of this. The credit of this invention is recorded in the name of Italian scientist G. Marconi. He was even awarded Nobel Prize in Physics (1909). Not only that it has now come to light that the sensitive detector that Marconi used for his transatlantic transmission in 1901 was in fact invented by Bose which Marconi never acknowledged. This has been brought to notice by US based institute of Electronics and Electrical Engineering (IEEE). Marconi used iron mercury iron Coherer with telephone detector invented by Bose in 1898. This was published in proceedings of the Royal Society, London on 27th April 1899; more than two years before Marconi's first wireless transmission between England and Newfoundland in Canada on 12th December 1901.

It is said that Marconi's childhood friend, Luigi Solari who was lieutenant with the Italians Navy; brought Bose's invention to the notice of Marconi. Ironically, Bose despite his important role, remained away from due credit. He wrote many letters from London to Rabindranath Tagore which amply illustrate the fact. Some contents are as follows... 'The authorities of a wireless telegraphic concern (Muirhead & Co) have received results beyond their expectations by producing instruments based on my theory... . About my further ideas on the subject he (head of the firm) begged me not to make things public but allow him to take out patents. But I cannot find heart to give any part of my life for money making purpose'. The letters clearly indicate Bose's aversion about patents despite financial constraints. Marconi on the other hand had often been accused of merely taking and utilizing other people's idea. He used to retort 'I doubt very much whether there has ever been a case of a useful invention in which all the theory, all the practical applications and all the apparatus were the work of one man'. It is indeed clever and cunning reply.

Bose's credentials were impeccable. He was renowned physicist. He was the first to generate extremely short radio waves that are called microwaves in 1895. He also studied their properties such as polarization using equipment he himself fabricated and designed. Of course, Bose did not continue the work on wireless and changed over to the study of plant life around 1900. He made world class discoveries, in this field too, using ultra sensitive self made instruments. In June 1997, there was symposium on microwaves at Denver, Colorado, USA. Several original instruments were demonstrated which were designed by Bose. Large audience reacted, such high fidelity instruments could have been developed with such meagre resources hundred years ago!" Along with Bose's name, work of Hertz and Helmholtz is also important in this regards. It is said that Lord Kelvin was so impressed by the work of Bose that in excitation—'not only broke into the warmest praise, but also limped upstairs in to the ladies' gallery to greet Mrs. Bose' It is worthwhile to quote Kipling's line in "The Ballad of East and West" "But there is neither east nor west, Border, nor Breed nor Birth" Bose the outstanding Indian had got the reorganisation worldwide as indicated in above line.

Bose is the most recognized scientist as botanist and biophysicist. He could prove that plants have life. They react to the atmosphere, they have feelings (pleasure, sorrow, healthy, diseased etc) It was difficult to accept these things in those days but now there is ample of evidence in this regard. It is proved that plants can react to music also. There is effect of heat and cold on plants. During night plants get contracted. Very minute movements to plants can be measured accurately. Bose devised such instruments like Crescograph (supersensitive instruments), resonant recorder, accelerating recorder, compound lever, balancing apparatus etc. He could notice the quivering of injured plants. Observations about lotus flower, sun flower are now routine. Bose minutely noticed the changes in these flowers. He also noticed changes in date tree. The cells in plant can also expand and contract. Interesting observation was about Mimosa plant (*Lajaloo* in *Devnagari*), if it is touched by finger or stick its leaves close down and afterwards they separate. He carried one experience to show effect of poison on the plants. The experiment was not successful because the bottle containing solution of poison was wrongly/purposely filled by water. The person who did this accepted the mistake as Bose tried to inject solution in the bottle in his body. Such was the courage and confidence of Bose. Many people tried to trouble Bose out of jealously. Two persons namely Walter and Sanderson were caught for the purpose. They did not allow Bose's paper to be published in Proceedings of Royal Society. Some of the papers were published in their names. Royal society also had some objections in these papers e.g. 'they were more philosophical'.

It is still a matter of debate 'How Life Originates?' Pasteur was the scientist who preferred 'life originate from life'. However when first lives had originated, they must be how inanimate material (non-living material) like water, nitrogen, methane etc. Recent researches about possibility of life on other planets like mars, moons etc. have roots in this thinking. Bose tried to put similar ideas about abolishing the difference between living and non-living. It was not accepted that time and even today. This was based on minute vibrations in plants, animals and also in non living matter. As frog leg responds to electrical shock for some time and after some time it stops reacting because of 'fatigue'. Such type of 'fatigue' is also observed in non-living objects like say spring. Spring elongates by force and when force is removed it regains its original shape, it elasticity. By repeated use of spring, spring also loose this property i.e. it gets fatigued some points like vibrations,. fatigue and others were correlated by Bose. Bose was blamed for having been carried away by a sort of enchantment exercised out of his own conjuring. For his use of words like fatigue, sleep, exaltation, irritability etc in respect of inert and vegetative matter was taken as illegitimate. His work however, remains much in reserve even today. The Encyclopaedia Britannica in his biographical note has nicely summed up his work as—"so much in advance of his time that its precise evaluation was not possible". This is wonderful contribution. There is open-endedness in his research.

As indicated above his research was not properly published or there were some difficulties. He therefore, published lot of his work in the form of books and also collected papers of himself were self edited (1927). His important books includes Plant Response (1906), Response in the Living and Non Living (1902), Electro—Physiology of Plants (1907), Irritability of Plants/ Life Movements of Plants(1904), The Physiology of Photosynthesis, The Nervous Mechanism of Plants (1926), The Motor Mechanism of Plants (1928), Traffic Movement and Growth of Plants etc. The titles of these books are self explanatory. This also indicates the vastness of his work.

Sir Bose had travelled a lot in the country and abroad. He had been twice to England in connection with his studies and research work. He also gave lectures with demonstrations in his lucid and interesting style in the countries like France, Germany, America and Japan. He was well received and praised at all these places. Bose was in the service of Presidency College from 1885 to 1915. He was granted special extension in service for two years 1913-15(Emeritus Professor). Later he started in 1917 Bose Research Institute. He was the Director of the institute right from its inception till his death. He tried to maintain high standard to the institute and its Indianness. He looked upon the institute as if it is the Temple of Knowledge/wisdom/ learning/ research. In front of the institute there is a statue of marching woman with torch (*mashal*) in her raised hand. It is carved in the institute that it is built for the glory of India and to impart the world of pleasure and satisfaction. It is dedicated to the God for this purpose. This indicated his views about institute in which values are important along with knowledge and its development.

J.C. Bose had good association with renowned people like Rabindranath Tagore, P.C. Ray, G.K. Gokhale, Mahatma Gandhi, Margaret Nobel (Bhagini Nividita), Vivekanand and alike in our country. He was also having good friends like Mrs. Bull, Barnard Shaw and French writer Roma Rola abroad. Shaw and Roma Rola have dedicated one book each to the friendship of Bose. Rabindranath Tagore has also dedicated one poem '*Karna Kunti Samwad*' (Dialogues between *Karna* and *Kunti* in Mahabharat) to J.C. Bose. Mrs Bull came in contact with Bose through Bhagini Nivedita. She looked after Bose in Europe when he was not well. She came all the way from America to do so. There were number of friends working in the scientific field especially in Botany and Physics.

Many honours were showered on J. C. Bose Cambridge University conferred him honorary degree of D. Sc. in 1896. He was nominated as Fellow of Royal Society in 1920. British Government knighted him as 'Sir' in 1916. He was also elected as Chairman of 'Bengal Sahitya Parishad' Bengal Literary association.

Bose was not well during last four years of his life span. He was shifted to Giridih in Bihar in order to change the atmosphere and to have rest. He worked till 22nd November 1937. He corrected the proofs of Journal of Bose Institute. He heard national songs '*Jan Gan Man Adhinayak..*' and '*Vande Matram...*' on gramophone in the night before going to bed. He collapsed in bathroom on 23rd November 1937 morning and expired there. Such is the touching life sketch of Nationalist Scientist Bose.

12
James Batcheller Sumner

With advancement of science and technology many times it is said that man has conquered the nature. Man is successful in taming the nature for his comforts and wills. It is however proved false occasionally. *e.g.* the earth quakes, unpredictable monsoon, volcanoes, unforeseen diseases, miraculous remedies by medical plants, unexplored flora and fauna and many other problems posed by nature really seem to be out of reach by human beings. It will be wise to say that man should have unending quest in co-operation with nature. The mysteries of nature can't be fully understood. More and more we are successful in solving them, they extend further more. Many chemical reactions which seem to be impossible in a laboratory can be carried out of by nature with ease and precision at very normal conditions. Plants produce carbohydrates using sunlight in presence of chlorophyll from the simple chemicals like water and carbon dioxide. Many natural drugs are obtained from plants which have very complicated structures like strychnine,

reserpine etc. Many metabolic processes occurring in living beings are chemical reactions carried out by nature's wonderful catalysts—enzymes. During recent years bio-chemistry and bio-technology have become fore front areas for research, unravelling many problems and getting better solutions. The history of bio-chemistry goes parallel with history of enzymes.

Enzymes are proteinous in nature. They catalyze many reactions in living cells. They are really wonderful and amazing entities. They are biocatalysts. They are very specific and carry most of the reactions at room temperature or body temperature and with normal condition like neutral environment (optimum pH about 7) few exceptional enzymes such as pepsinogen and trypsin have optimum activity at pH 5.2 (mild acidic) and 7.8 (very mild basic) respectively. Pepsinogen is an inactive enzyme. It is activated into pepsin by dilute hydrochloric acid present in gastric juice. Pepsin breaks down proteins into peptides. Similar is the role of trypsin. This is just to illustrate the point. In extreme acidic and basic medium enzymes usually get deactivated. Enzymes have the ability to accelerate the rates of reactions many fold. The specificity of enzymes is absolutely remarkable. They have wide varieties of specificity like substrate stereo etc. There are innumerable enzymes. Though most of them are proteins, we now know that certain R.N.A (RiboNucleic Acids) molecules can also act as enzymes. The 1989 Nobel Prize for chemistry went to Sidney Altman (of Yale University) and Thomas R. Cech (of University of Colorado, Boulder) for this discovery. RNA is prominently involved in the synthesis of enzymes and other proteins where as other nucleic acids (DNA DeoxyRiboNucleic Acids) are responsible for the storage of generic information and heredity.

The reactions which cannot be carried out with sophisticated equipments and highly skilled manpower can be carried out with ease by enzymes. These are magic molecules of nature, giant in size and versatile. With the name enzyme other name is associated and that is of James Batcheller Sumner. He was working with enzyme urease and for the first time he was able to isolate it in pure crystalline form and characterize it as a protein. It was the great achievement in enzymology.

Sumner was born on 19th November 1887 at Canton, Massachusetts USA. His father was Charles Sumner and mother was Elizabeth Rand Sumner. They were engaged in manufacturing business and forming also. The family was well to do and Sumner could get his education with comfort. He was graduated from Howard College in 1910 with Chemistry as his subject. He worked in his uncle's textile plant for sometime. He also worked as a teacher at Sackville (Mt. Allison College) in 1911. He accepted an assistantship in chemistry at the Worcester Polytechnic Institute. He left it next year to study biochemistry at the Howard Medical School. Sumner received his Ph. D. in 1914. The title of his thesis was "The Formation of Urea in the Animal Body." His supervisor was O. Folin and he worked in association with C.H. Fiske. In 1914 he accepted the position of assistant professor of bio chemistry at the Cornell Medical School. He was made full professor in 1929. In 1930 he became member of the Zoology Department and that of the Department of Bio-chemistry and nutrition at Cornell. In 1947, separate laboratory for Enzyme Chemistry was established and Sumner became his first Director. Sumner worked at Carnell till his retirement on 1st July 1955.

During his tenure Sumner travelled to Sweden to work on enzymes with Hans Van Euler-Chelpin at the University of Stockholm and Svedberg at the University of Uppsala. Sumner has to work with heavy teaching duties and during early years with inadequate laboratory facilities. He and his colleagues used to pray for cold weather for their cooling and crystallization experiments. They used to keep their beakers, conical flasks, test tubes for cooling in window/edges. Sumner had exceptionally good hand for practical laboratory techniques. He was a popular teacher and used to make his lectures interesting by personal anecdotes. His thinking was concrete. He used to get quick results, many times unexpected by brilliant flashes of intuition rather than long laborious process envisaged by other people. Many times he would work furiously without any result. His manners were often abrupt and difficult to get on. He was however kind hearted and human really. He was proud of his accomplishments.

Diastase was the first enzyme that was isolated by the French chemist Anselme Payen in 1833. The enzymes were many times equated to yeast which was responsible for conversion of starch to sugar to Alcohol. Chemical nature of enzymes was the matter of disputes by 1920. On the contrary German chemist Richard Willstaetter had produced negative evidence to the effect that enzymes were neither carbohydrates nor lipids or proteins. Willstaetter was the great personality and he got Nobel Prize in 1915 for his work on Chlorophyll. Against this background Sumner began his studies of enzyme urease in 1917. He took urease for the purpose because he had earlier experience with it; secondly the enzyme could be established quantitatively by measuring the amount of ammonia and carbon dioxide evolved and thirdly rich source of urease the jack bean (*Canavalia ensiformis*) was available. Urease is the enzyme which converts urea to ammonia and carbon dioxide. Sumner tried to analyse jack bean and found many components in it. In his attempts to concentrate and purify urease, he found that 30% alcoholic extracts of jack bean contained more urease and was comparatively more pure. Undissolved portion contained unwanted proteins and other things. He obtained less pure samples of urease from alcoholic extracts at low temperature. By intuitional flash, he changed the solvent from alcohol to acetone. He extracted jack bean by 30% acetone and cooled the extract. He could not get crystals but when the extract way seen under microscope tiny crystals of new shape (octahedral) were noticed. The extract was centrifuged and some crystals were obtained. These were water soluble and showed test for protein and had very high urease activity. This was the great discovery and "for his discovery that enzymes can be crystallized". He was later awarded Nobel Prize in 1946 in sharing with J.N. Northrup and W.M. Stanley. Sumner got half the prize and Northrup Stanley got other half. Major share was with Sumner.

He was struggling for crystallization for nine years from 1917 to 1926. Sumner's views were not accepted by scientific community dominated by views of Willstaetter. Willstaetter used to say that enzymes were low molecular weight substances absorbed upon such carrier colloids and proteins. There way acrimony controversy on Sumner's work. There was suspicious feeling about Sumner's work at German University of Prague. How person was able to accomplish something which German could not! From 1926 to 30 there were many publications in support of Sumner's work. In 1930 J.N. Northup announced isolation of enzyme pepsin in the crystalline forms. He also crystallized trypsin (1932) and chymotrypsin (1935). Hereafter merit of Sumner's work began to be recognized. In 1937 Sumner and his students A.L. Dounce carried out crystallization of enzyme catalase. The proteinous nature was also substantially proved. Further peroxidoses, Lipoxidases and other enzymes were obtained.

Sumners career is the nice example of the persistence of investigator who stubbornly treads a path that his more influential contemporaries considered to be a blind alley. Later it was proved that they were wrong and Sumner way right. Sumner retained certain amount of embitterment for the unjustified criticism in his life.

Sumner's other striking and motivating point was he had no left hand. He carried many things which couldn't be imagined by his only right hand. It is more striking because he was left handed. In his early age he lost the hand in shooting accident. He was enthusiastic hunter. He still remained throughout his life a good sportsman—a tennis player. He was fond of skiing, sailing and hiking. Many people tried to distract his attention from research as he had no left hand. He had strong will power and determination. He learnt whole heartedly to do everything and that too with great skill with right hand. He succeeded in his achievements and therefore it is the great lesson to be learnt from him.

The mysterious side of Sumner's life was his three marriages. His first marriage took place in 1915 with Bertha Ricketts. He took divorce in 1930. He had five children from her. He then had second marriage and it could also not last long. His third marriage took place in 1943 with Mary Morrison and they had two children. His relations with his wife appeared to be cordial and he used to take keen interest in all his household activities, tours and excursions. The divorces might be due to abrupt and little eccentric nature of Sumner. Many a time he used to be furious and overactive. He had internal pinch of salt in his mind that his accomplishments were unnecessarily criticized and this might had resulted in non-adjusting nature. Whatever may be the reason he remained little less understood as the person. His nature was as complex as his scientific field namely enzymes.

Sumner's work stimulated further research in the enzyme field and the related field of viruses and viral diseases like influenza. His further work was with enzyme aiding the digestive processes. This laid the foundation for new research in nutrition. Lot of work is now going on in nutrition. The branch has acquired full fledged status. Sumner made it possible to accelerate studies of bio catalysis. He remained active and physically fit till few months before his death. He died on 12th August 1935 at Buffalo, New York.

Sumner will be ever remembered for his contributions in enzyme field, intuition, single handedness, sportive nature, unjustifiable criticism and mysterious personal life.

13

Shrinivas Ramanujan

The greatest mathematical genius in the modern times about whom every Indian should be proud of is Shrinivas Ramanujan. His life was full of brilliant flashes of intelligence, dynamic and short lived; which is why more touching and lingering in the minds of all intelligentsia forever. It is probably the unique example of achieve appreciation if the talent born in India and fully recognized and nourished in western country like England. Prof G.H. Hardy and Littlewood are two persons who are to be noted on front line about this. We talk about 'brain drain' because of better facilities, more money and conducive atmosphere and devoted and engrossed colleagues abroad. The basic need of genius however is free and open surroundings with great potential to express one self. It is also necessary that couple of people should be able to understand to smaller or greater extent and have a potential to interact with new ideas, insight and creativity. Ramanujan could get this because of G.H. Hardy. Hardy in turn had same feeling about Ramanujan. It is quoted

'If it had not been for Ramanujan collaboration the 1914-18 war would have been darker for Hardy than it was'.

Ramanujan was born on Thursday 22nd December 1887 at Erode near Kumbhakonam in Tamil Nadu. His mother (Komalamma) and father (Shrinivas Aiyangar) were devoted Hindus. They were quite simple, honest and cultured people. His father was the clerk with one cloth merchant and straight forward modest man. His mother was clever and stern. They were worshippers of Goddess *Namagiri* of Namakkal in Salem District. It was said that Ramanujan was the gift of that Goddess. He was named as Ramajuan since Shri Ramanujan Acharya, one of the best profounder of *Vishisht Advait*a philosophy was also born on Thursday. His mother used to call him China Swami which means little Lord.

Ramanujan had his early education in Kumbhakonam. It is Prayag of south where Mahamakham, a function resembling the kumbhmela is held once in 12 years. He passed in 1897 primary school certificate examination and stood first in Tanjawar district. He passed in 1903 Matric examination critical questions with long and studied answers used to be asked. In such examination to score marks was very difficult Ramanujan could get first class was remarkable thing. He could get junior Subramanyam Scholarship for further study at the Government College at Kumbhakonam. When he was studying for the first year in college, he was totally engrossed in mathematics and neglected other subjects as a result he failed for the first year. This made him leave Kumbhakonam first for Vishkhapatanam and then for Madras and he return back to Kumbhakonam after. He attempted first year examination for the second time but again failed. He spent next few years studying mathematics independently. Ramanujan got married to Janaki on 14th July 1909. It become necessary now to search a job for him.

Ramanujan contacted Principal Sheshu Ayyar of Kumbhakonam college in connection with job and with two bulky notebooks in which he had his theorems of mathematics. Ayyar was much impressed by his work of mathematics and gave him temporary appointment in the office of accountant general at Madras. Ayyar also recommended him the Journal of Indian Mathematical Society and encouraged him to contribute for this journal. He wrote his first paper entitled 'Some properties of Bernoulli numbers'. It was a long and elaborate paper of 14 pages and 9 questions.

Sheshu Ayyar directed Ramanujan to meet Diwan Bahadur R. Ramachandra Rao, the then collector of Nellor, a small town, some 125 km north from Madras. Rao was a great admirer of mathematics and was also much impressed by Ramanujan's work. Some of the sentences in own words of Rao about his first meeting with Ramanujan are worth quoting—'A short uncouth figure, stout, unshared, not over clean, with one conspicuous feature-shining eyes—walked in with frayed notebook under his arm. He was miserably poor. He had run away from Kumbhakonam to get leisure in Madras to pursue his studies. He never craved for any distinction, he wanted leisure; in other words, that simple food should be provided for him without exertion on his part and that he should be allowed to dream on'.

He opened his book and began to explain some of his discoveries. I saw quite at once that there was something out of the ways but my knowledge did not permit me to judge whether he talked sense or non-sense... And then he had gauged my ignorance and showed me some of his simpler results. These transcended existing books and I had no doubt that he was remarkable man. Then step by step he led me to elliptic integrals and hyper geometric series and at last his theory of divergent series and at last his theory of divergent series not yet announced to the world converted me. I asked him what he wanted. He said he wanted a pittance to live on so that he might pursue his researches. Rao then supported him for some time but Ramanujan was not willing to live on somebody's help indefinitely. He was unwilling to exist on charity. He finally got a job in 1912 at Madras Port Trust. Ramanujan was happy therefore and could concentrate on mathematics at his saved time and leisure time.

Ramanujan had very high mathematical ability since his childhood. He had read Loney's Trignometry while he was still a student of 8th class. He also came across Carr's book 'Synopsis of Elementary Results in Pure and Applied Mathematics' 2 volumes (1880-86). In these books points earlier to 1860 were discussed. This book had 6165 theorems/ results in various branches of mathematics. These books had a profound influence on the subsequent development of Ramanujan.

Ramanujan had startling knowledge of mathematics. His work on

1. Continued fractions is unequalled
2. Riemann Series
3. The elliptic integrals
4. hyper geometric series
5. the functional equations of Zeta functions
6. Own theory of divergent series etc are worth noting.

Similarly his gaps in knowledge of mathematics were equally startling. He was not aware of the basic formal points like mathematical proof. In his theory of prime numbers many theorems were wrong. He used to refer that he dreamed the formulae and when he was awake he used to write them on papers. As he had no formal education in mathematics, the things strike him spontaneously and naively. It is real genius. Intuition was the primary force of the knowledge he had or created. He had nice natural instinct. As a result for his phenomenal genius he was the 1st Indian to be nominated as the Fellow of Royal society of London in 1918. He was only compared with Euler (1707-83) and Jacobi (1804-51). Such was his outstanding accomplishments which any other peer worker had not at his credit.

While Ramanujan was serving at the Port Trust he was receiving encouragement from many people including the manager of Trust—Narain Iyer, chairman of Trust—Sir Francis Spring, Prof. Middlemax of Presidency college, Madras, Prof. Griffith of Government Engineering college, Madras, Bourne—Director of Public instruction, W. Graham- the Accountant General of Madras, Sir Gilbert walker—Director General of Observatories in Simla who was on a visit to Madras. Gilbert was also fellow of Royal Society of London. Sir Gilbert wrote a letter to Francis Didsbury the then registrar of Madras University recommending him to provide a place to Ramanujan in the University. As Ramanujan was not having formal degree of the University, the case was referred to the governor Lord Pentland and Ramanujan was granted a scholarship of Rs: 75/- per month for two years. He was also granted leave for two years by the Port Trust with effect from 1st May 1913. Ramanujan joined the university as the first research scholar. These details very well explain that Ramanujan's integrity with mathematics and his capacities were par excellence. He was also unassuming and quite simple, therefore, people whole-heartedly extended full co-operation spontaneously.

Ramanujan wrote Prof. G.H. Hardy of Cambridge his first letter on January 16, 1913. As he read the book written by Hardy namely—Orders of Infinity. In his letter, he also enclosed his work in mathematics. Prof. Hardly received that script at noon time. 'The script appeared to consist of theorems, most of them wild or fantastic looking, one or two already well known, laid out as thought they were original. There were no proofs of any kind. There were theorems such as he had never seen before, not imagined, Hardy was not only bored but irritated. He kept the script aside but the trail of thoughts lingered in his mind. Prof Hardy and Prof. Littlewood then studied the script in greater detail at night and realized the greatness of the author and decided to have him in England.

Ramanujan could get scholarship of 250 pounds a year for two years from 1st April 1914. Ramanujan sailed for England on 17th March 1914 by boat named Newasa. He reached to England on 14th April and Trinity College Cambridge on 18th April. During journey also Ramanujan was busy with his theorems and imaginations. He worked in England from 1914 to 1918—4 years. Earlier in India also he could carry out good research from 1907 to 1911—4 years. Total 8 years research was very important. He published many research papers of high value. These papers have opened up new era for the researchers and the process still continues.

There were many difficulties for his going to England. The family was orthodox. Many religious organizations vehemently opposed his going, even his mother. It is said that his mother Komalamma dreamt that her son was amongst the distinguished foreigners arguing on some points. People were patiently listening him and gave loud applause. Goddess also gave positive indications for his going abroad in mother's dream and thus finally he was allowed to go.

In 1916 Ramanujan was awarded the B.A. degree of Cambridge University. In 1918, he was elected a fellow of the Trinity College Cambridge. Many honours were for him. In 1917 Ramanujan fell ill and had to be admitted to a nursing home in Putney. Hardy went to Putney for meeting him by taxi cab whose number was 1729—dull number. During discussion he remarked about that number—'It is the smallest number expressible as the sum of two cubes in two different ways'

$$1729 = 1^3 + 12^3 = 1 + 1728$$

$$1729 = 9^3 + 10^3 = 729 + 1000$$

He had a wonderful insight about the numbers and their correlations e.g.

$$2^5 * 9^2 = 2592$$

$$3^{3*} * 7^3 * 1^3 = 371$$

He could get value of π up to 31 decimal points.

$\pi = (63/25)\,((17 + 15\sqrt{5})/(7 + 15\sqrt{5}))$ could give values points. He could prepare magic squares within no time and can give the formulae and equations to do so.

13	46	27	14
10	31	39	20
41	11	19	29
36	12	15	37

100 sum 4 columns

17	24	1	8	15
23	5	7	14	16
4	6	13	20	22
10	12	19	21	3
11	18	25	2	9

65 sum 5 columns

1	49	41	33	25	17	9
18	10	2	43	42	34	26
35	27	19	11	3	44	36
45	37	29	28	20	12	4
13	5	46	38	30	22	21
23	15	14	6	47	39	31
40	32	24	16	8	7	48

175 sum 7 columns

These are just three examples recorded in his own hand writing.

He could conclude that any number can be expressed by maximum 4 squares and their sum.

$$7 = 2^2 + 1^2 + 1^2 + 1^2$$

$$15 = 3^2 + 2^2 + 1^2 + 1^2 \text{ etc.}$$

$$\text{Number} = x^2 + y^2 + z^2 + u^2$$

$$= ax^2 + by^2 + cz^2 + du^2$$

Ramanujan could give 55 different set of values for a, b, c, d. i.e. 1,1,1,1 as for 15 above. It could be also 1, 1, 1, 4.

$$15 = 3^2 + 1^2 + 1^2 + 4^2 \text{ etc}$$

Some more examples of numbers and presentation can be given

$$31 = 6n + 1 \qquad n = 5$$

$$= X^2 + 3Y^2 = 2^2 + 3*3^2 = 4 + 27$$

$$31 = 30n + 1 \qquad n = 1$$

$$= x^2 + 15y^2 = 4^2 + 15*\ 1^2 = 16 + 15 \text{ etc.}$$

His work related to modular equations, approximation to π, high composite numbers definite integrals etc is of great value. Our main sources for Ramanujan's research contributions are the following :

1. The three quarterly reports submitted by him to Madras University;
2. His 37 published papers and 58 questions and solutions—collected papers published by Cambridge University Press (1927) 5 papers were published before going to England;
3. Ramanujan's Note Books. Published by Tata Institute of Fundamental Research TIFR (1953);
4. The lost note book discovered by Prof. George E. Andrews in 1976 and published in 1987 by Narosa Publishers, New Delhi.

Ramanujan was equally great as a human being as that of mathematician. He was very simple and modest. He loved his family and he wanted to have pleasant and joyful atmosphere in the house. Whenever he was free from his mathematics, he would like to chit chat with the members of his family. He used to tell the stories from the religious ancient literature of Hindus or strange stories. He was also witty and would try to narrate turns from mathematics. He preferred to prepare his own meals when he was in England. He used to like milk, fruits, rice and curry of gram (pulses) flour (*Pitla*). He was hospitable and many Indians like C.D. Deshmukh and P.C. Mahalanobis had experienced this. In India when he was much engrossed in his work, he used to write formulae and equations work, he used to write formulae and equations by right hand with pencil on paper and at the same time his mother used to server him food on left hand that he used to eat mechanically.

He had natural sympathy for poor and downtrodden students. He encouraged them for learning actively by giving them fees etc. He however was self taught. He used to get the pleasure and joy in others successes. However, he accepted his own successes, honours and felicitations indifferently and with saint like mentality. His English friends used to call him as JAM, really he was the GEM of the persons.

In 1917 Ramanujan fell ill and his illness grew from bad to worse. He was sent back to India in 1919. He arrived at Madras on 2nd April 1919 and passed away a year later on 26th April 1920 at Cheptet near Madras. He had very short life of just 32-33 years. Even on his death bed he devoted himself completely to mathematics.

He will be ever remembered for his outstanding contributions to number theory and analysis and new vistas for research. More touching points about him are without formal training, without any means of support and even at the face of death he continued to work of highest order.

14

George Washington Carver

'Start where you are, with what you have. Make something of it. Never be satisfied.' This is the thing that was practised by Carver throughout his life. This message was eternal and he made the life of slave Negros something worth living for. Carver's life is the ideal life that was lived for others especially to the class of society which was downtrodden and under the shackles of slavery, ignorance and without self confidence. Carver will be ever remembered for his awaking and motivating work, dedication, sacrifice and humble approach. He was described as partly saint, partly scientist and partly performing bear (He was careless about his dress and presentation, people wanted always to push him for the purpose. He preferred to work by himself and avoid publicity). The sentence on his tomb clearly represents his philosophy of life—'He could have added fortune to fame but caring for neither, he found happiness and honour in being helpful to the world.' In a sense he was

messenger of God for the upliftment of poor and innocent lot of Negros.

There is no certainty about Carver's date of birth. The calculated (speculated) date of birth is 12 July 1861. He was born to the Negro slave parents. His father was killed in the accident and he was living with his mother at Diamond Grove in extreme south west corner of Missouri. The estate at Diamond Grove was owned by Moses Carver (German) and his wife Susan Carver. Mary was the name of Carver's mother. She was taken away by the invaders and Moses could keep back George Carver after negotiations with them and in place of horse worth 300 dollars. As a child he was quite weak, frail and sick. He was suffering from nursing gesture that could keep Carver going on. He was nature lover from the beginning. His observation capacity was astonishing. He could prepare bird's nest exactly the same way as birds do it. One could not believe that it was prepared by human being. He was just a part of nature as plants, trees, shrubs, birds, animals etc. living harmoniously. It is said that 'Knowledge comes but wisdom lingers' But in Carver's case there was inborn wisdom that was inherited from God almighty. Moses Carver asked George to look after garden, pet animals and courtyard. He could do it so nicely and with enthusiasm. He could keep on hours together watching the development of plants, insects, butterflies, diseases on plants and alike. Soon he was nick named as 'small gardener'. Because of his small stature he could not do hard work with Moses but could help his nursing mother Susan in every household work. In Carver's family two things were deeply inculcated in his young mind—one was neatness, discipline and cleanliness and second was 'live most economically'! Without wastage, luxuries and only need based. He kept him busy in wool spinning, handicrafts washing, cooking, sewing, preserving food, carving, painting, tanning leather, preparing pudding, masala and candles etc. He was versatile assistance to any nice house wife. He was invited for the purpose by many. He could do the things in most nice way and could cast lasting impression on the minds of people. 'Work' and 'Work in the best possible manner' was his nature. He was quite dependable young child. Once Swiss agriculturist Hermann Langer visited Missouri State to study the possibility of grape cultivation, he tried out some experiments at Carver's estate at Diamond

Grove and found it to be suitable for grapes. During the period young George Carver proved to be the best asset for sensitive grape cultivation. George could care grape field with utmost precautions and for healthy development. This clearly indicated his aptitude for botany and agriculture.

George left Carver's estate for Neosho when he was just 10 years old with meagre belongings like old shawl, half cut pant of Moses, two books (books of arithmetic and that given by Jaegar) and cutting blade for plants. This was his first journey in pursuits and propagation of knowledge. He passed very difficult time at Neosho and could hardly survive the bitter winter. He worked for survival and tried to learn. He was fortunate to get in contact with John Martin and his wife at Neosho. They treated George with love and affection. Martins took him to the church and many places. He was made little social by then. He also was brought in contact with Maria and her husband Andy uncle. With these two families George could learn lot and had little comfortable school days. He left in 1876 for 'Fort Scot. During his departure Maria gave George one copy of 'Bible' which was preserved by him life-long. At Fort Scot he could get many bitter experiences but he accepted them with cheerful heart and as necessary reinforcement for life. He started one laundry there and it became quite popular. He completed his high school in Minneapolis in 1885. He was first informed about the admission in Highland University but later on refused the admission because of his Negro origin. This was just like 'nipping in bud experience. Still he kept on. During his frustrated period once he went to church and sang, his singing was so melodious and heart warming that he could catch the eye of MilHolland family. By MilHolland family's recommendations George decided to take admission in Simpson College, Indianola, Iowa. Simpson college gave new meaning and purpose to the life to George. He made many wonderful drawings there under the guidance of Mr. Bud. Out of these 27 drawings are still preserved in 'Carver Art Collection. Drawing and Music were his two pet likings along with plant cultivations. He left the Simpson College and took admission in state agricultural college at Ames, Iowa in Botany and soil chemistry department, in 1891. There also he worked hard in various ways and became popular as 'ideal student. He participated in military education also. He got the rank of Captain. Probably, he must be the first negro student to get this rank. He got his bachelor's degree on 1894 and masters degree in 1896. He had opportunity to work with Louis Pammell noted botanist and mycologist. The way of his education was through all thorny area with little oasis in the farm of different families that came across his ways.

After his education he got a job and could have obtained better and high paid jobs anywhere. The speciality of Carver was he reacted to the call of Booker T. Washington from Alabama. He was running 'Tuskegee Normal and industrial school for Negros'. He took over as the director and instructor in Scientific Agriculture and Diary Science. He started his career on 8th October 1896 with salary of 125 dollars a month. It remained the fixed salary throughout his life. The mission was undertaken by Carver because he wanted to uplift his Negro brothers and sisters. There could not be better person that Carver to do this job. Carver belonged to that class, he was knowing the pulse of people and remained linked to these people throughout. Carver had knowledge, necessary wisdom and intuition. He had learnt the art of teaching and his approach was to inculcate the knowledge slowly which was much in tune with people.

When Carver joined the school of Alabama, it was barren place. There were hardly any shrubs or plants nearby the school. In Alabama, people used to take continuous crop of cotton. The soil therefore had lost its fertility, texture and utility. People were worried. The first thing that Carver did was to improve the quality of the soil. This was done by substituting cropping pattern in place of single crop. The crops were taken alternately cotton, peanut or groundnut, sweet potato and soyabean. The three new crops that were proposed were to improve the nitrogen content of the soil and humus content also (organic carbon). These plants were nitrogen producing legumes. On the roots of these plants there are granular growths which fix nitrogen in the soil. Soya bean was cultivated and then buried in the soil to get organic fertilizer for the soil. People were made aware of this scientific fact and 'farmer organisation' was formed. It was sharing of experiences and mutually get benefited by the experiences of all. Many farmers who were not able to come to Tuskegee could get the information and knowledge required to them at their door steps. The 'mobile laboratory and school' was set up for the benefits of farmer. The van with expertise and modern techniques and processes would move from places to places demonstrating the use of different things. Food and food products were also demonstrated. People slowly got into the stream and changed their single crop pattern to multi crop pattern. They also allowed some part of soil to burn the soil as they were doing earlier. The burning destroys hums. They started using compost fertilizers.

Many misconcepts were rooted in the minds of people. For example tomato was considered as poisonous fruit. They were not using it. Carver demonstrated its utility and effective use in various farms. There were deaths of some cows, Carver found out the reason that it was due to Rattle Box—Crotalaria the poisonous grass eaten by cows. Carver tried all the way to cultivate the minds of farmers scientifically and with lot of factual information at the base. There were no vagueness in approach but clear cut results and observations for their support.

People realized the importance of Carver's views and cultivated large amount of peanuts, sweet potatoes and soya bean, this resulted in surplus supplies and cost radically went down. This adversely affected Carver's approach. Carver, however, demonstrated processing on peanuts and sweet potatoes that led to number of products. He was able to demonstrate about 300 products from peanuts and 118 products from sweet potatoes. As a result carver was also nicknamed as 'Peanut man'. The products included plastics, dyes, medicines, flour, powder milk, wood strains, fertilizers curing agent for plant diseases and soil builders. The eatable products had different tastes and could not be recognized that they were made up of peanuts or sweet potatoes. As a result the economy of Alabama was radically changed and people could live comfortably and their standard for living slowly increased. They took education and brought themselves in the mainstream of civilized American life. This was Carver's great accomplishment. Along with these three crops Carver also studied thousands of plants and their utility as medicinal plants or otherwise. His first publication was 'Feeding Acorns to Livestock' (1898). It was followed by 43 other publications of useful value and research potential. Demonstration, exhibition and 'practice first and then preach' remained the strategy of Carver's teaching along with useful research. In his opinion nothing was waste, it was only the form that matters. He therefore prepared may useful and important articles from so-called 'waste'. For example instead of linseed oil he used thrown motor oil. He used peanut oil for unknown use on paralysis. Roots of many plants were extracted and the extract was used for medicinal purposes. It was known that cotton crop was usually attacked by one type of disease in which the cotton buds get dropped. Calcium arsenate was the answer to the problem but carver could demonstrate that if peanut was cultivated nearby cotton, it could be avoided. He developed the science called Chemurgy. In this detailed analysis was done of the natural product and required permutations and combinations were done to suite the purpose of utility. Natural products thus could be blended and modified for variety for uses. He noticed that at some places of Alabama, soil could serve as natural colour. He prepared 'royal blue' colour from that soil and painted whole church building by that colour. Many natural colours and paints were extracted and utilized for drawings and paintings with outstanding and everlasting effects. World famous Ajanta and Ellora caves had been painted with such natural colours. Carver's work was similar but by using chemical analysis and scientific studies in greater detail. Pig fat and stove black was used as boot polish. People in south used to suffer from the diseases like Pellagra and Scurvy. It was concluded that these diseases were due to deficiency of some important food ingredients in the meals. The people used to mainly take three types of food-'3M' as it used to be said (Meat. Mill (flour) and Molasses). The deficiency could be met out by cereals, citrus fruits, peanut and sweet potato. Such was varied work of George W. Carver.

Carver remained bachelor throughout his life. There were some emotional and friendly relations between Miss. Hunt and Carver. It never materialized into marriage. Both of them found their lives to be more useful for others rather than for personal pleasures and family set up. Carver was in contact with renowned persons like Henry Ford, Thomas Alva Edison, Shri Huston. These people tried to participate in Carver's undertaking. Huston gave one 'diamond' at Carver's demand. He thought that Carver required it for his personal use but later on it was found in permanent exhibition. Edison offered him job worth 1 lakh dollars a year but Carver declined to accept the job because he never wanted to leave Tuskegee.

Carver's work brought him many awards, honours and medals. He got Spingarn Medal in 1923, Roosevelt Medal in 1939 and Thomas A. Edison Foundation Award in 1942. He was elected to British Royal Society of Arts in 1916 and Hall of Fame for great Americans in 1933. In 1940 Carver Research Foundation was established. Carver Museum was set up in 1941. The small wooden shed in Moses Carver's estate at Diamond Grove is preserved as national monument in the honour of George W. Carver. Carver did not accept any obligation in the form of material wealth right from his childhood. He tried to compensate it by hard work, help, drawings, paintings, cooking etc. He remained utterly grateful to those who tried to shape his life. People at large would all the time remain grateful for Carver's work. There is no certainty about his birth date because he was an insignificant then but his deeds are such a great that his passing away date is celebrated as Carver's day (5th June 1943).

15

Alexander Fleming

Penicillin is referred as the miracle/wonder drug because it has saved millions of lives. It is very effective against pneumonia, meningitis, veneral diseases and blood poisoning; and so many other diseases. It is devastating to variety of bacteria but almost harmless to the human or animal body. It is one of the most popular antibiotics. Antibiotics are chemical substances, produced by some micro organisms and which interfere with the growth and metabolism of other micro organisms. Antibiotics are thus chemotherapeutic agents and can be effective at very low concentrations.

Penicillin can be obtained in at least six different varieties by natural processes. When penicillin is used as the term what is generally referred to is the most common variety of penicillin that is benzyl penicillin or penicillin-II or G. It is obtained from mould 'penicillium notatum' or 'penicillium chrysogenum'. The preparation of penicillin thus involves cultivating above moulds in a suitable culture medium and extracting the penicillin produced either in a pure form or the solution that can be directly used. Penicillin has changed the medicinal field drastically.

With Penicillin, the name associated is of Dr. Alexander Fleming. He was bacteriologist. Fleming was very individual in his ideas and work. He however was simple and modest. He was keenly interested in other people and devoted much of his time and attention to them. He was annoyed by pomposity. He discovered penicillin but his approach was—'I didn't do anything invent penicillin. Nature makes penicillin I just found it by accident.' Such was this great man. He travelled over the world. He could capture the audience by his good humoured wits and modesty.

Alexander Fleming was born in Ayrshire. It was 4 miles from Darvel, in south west Scotland. His date of birth is 6 August 1981. Fleming's father was typical Scottish farmer. His life was very strenuous. He married twice. He had two daughters and two sons by his first marriage and one daughter and three sons by his second. Alexander was the second son of his father's second marriage. He was the youngest but one of all eight children. His mother was Grace Morton, the daughter of neighbouring farmer. Alexander was known as 'Alec' to his family and friends. When Alec was seven years old his father died. His mother was then virtually the head of the family. She managed the farm and family. She was an excellent and cheerful mother and a good cook. She was always enthusiastic in joining indoor games and fun. She kept the family jubilant and ongoing.

The Flemings were traditionally accustomed to securing a living from difficult land. They could not survive in their environment without closely watching field, stock and weather. They had deepened general knowledge of nature. They met adversity with silent resistance. Alec therefore had silent habits and in his mature years he regretted his lack of facility in verbal expression. He however expressed, 'I think I was fortunate in being brought up as a member of large family. We had no money to spend and there was nothing to spend money on. We had to make our own arrangements but that is easy in such surroundings. We had the farm animals and the trout in burns. We unconsciously learned a great deal about nature much of which is missed by a 'town dweller'.

Alec began to go to school at the age of five. He spent five years in the village school. He learned easily. He was at the heart a naturalist. His love for nature and automatic observation of living things, ultimately led him to his great discovery. At the age of ten he was sent to the school at Darvel. He used to walk between his farm house and Darvel—4 miles each way, to attend his school. Then he joined secondary school—Kilmarnock Academy, sixteen miles away. It was efficient school and more stress was on frequent examinations. He could learn there how to answer examination papers nicely. Alec's half brother Thomas was qualified in Medicine at Glasgow and established a practice in London. He almost behaved as a father for family. Alec followed him at the age of fourteen to London in 1895. At sixteen it was necessary for Alec to earn his living. He became a junior clerk in shipping firm. He used to copy documents, keep accounts and record details of cargo and passengers. He also joined, London Scottish volunteers in 1900. He became very good in rifle shoot. He enjoyed social, sporting, athletic and camping sides of their activities. He was the member of water polo team. He had thus an opportunity to develop various abilities in him.

Fortunately in 1901, he received a small legacy from his uncle who died. Alec did the work of shipping clerk satisfactorily but he found it quite dull. The legacy provided means for further education. He joined medicine. He showed usual ability and got senior entrance scholarship in natural science. Fleming was a brilliantly successful student. He won many prizes and got qualified in 1906. In 1908 he gained honours in six subjects in examination for his medical degree. He was also awarded the University's Gold Medal. He joined St. Mary's Hospital. In that hospital Almorth Wright was the Chairman of pathology department. This remarkable Irishman had already introduced inoculation against typhoid fever. Wright was convinced that the body contained many systems of self protection. One of it was disease eating white blood corpuscles. They are called phagocytes—the swallower cells. They swallow and digest bacteria. Wright linked the capacity of these cells to a special type of substance in blood fluid that he called as 'Opsonin' The measurement of a Person's Opsonin index for a given disease could be used to measure the strength of his resistance for that disease. Wright had substantially contributed towards quantitative medicine. He was also natural leader and rebel. Fleming and many of the best students were devoted to him. Fleming was influenced by Wright. He gave most loyal and devoted service. Fleming joined Wright's staff and began to work in his laboratory after securing his first medical qualification (1906). He further passed in 1909 Surgeon's examination.

Wright tried to establish strong connection between scientific research and clinical treatment. Fleming could get varied experience and intellectual creative atmosphere. It was a sort of academy, in night times many talented people used to gather and discuss. George Bernard Shaw was amongst these people. He wrote the drama 'The Doctor's Dilemma' having Wright in mind as the hero. Fleming in earlier years worked with White blood corpuscles and power of the body's self protecting systems impressed him deeply, it framed the main features of his thinking later on.

Before the First World War, Fleming produced a vaccine for the treatment of acne, the annoying pimples which caused so much psychological problems to young people. Paul Ehrich discovered all problems to young people. Paul Ehrich discovered 'salvarsan' for the treatment of syphilis (Germany). Ehrlich sent the first specimen to England for Wright for testing. It was in turn given to Fleming. Fleming was the first doctor in England to apply salvarsan. He became an authority in treating syphilis.

During First World War many people were wounded. Their treatment became a great problem. Conventional antiseptic-carbolic acid was found to be useful in preventing the infection of clean wounds and in treating wounds in which infection was not advanced. In rest of the cases patients died of gas gangrene and blood poisoning. Fleming studied the problem and found that carbolic acid was doing more harm to the white corpuscles and not to the dangerous micro organisms. He in this way studied many chemical antiseptics. His conclusion was all of them were liable to do more harm to the protective systems of the body than to the dangerous micro organisms they were intended to destroy. He returned to civil life with deepened suspicion of chemical antiseptics. He believed that biological antiseptics could be superior. He returned to St. Mary's Hospital.

He however did not resume his private practice but was now more interested in advancing medical knowledge than in repeating routine treatments.

Fleming got married on 23rd December 1915 in London with Sarah Morison McElroy an Irish lady. She used to be called by name Sally or Sareen. She was energetic outgoing person. She was talk active and cheerful. Alec on the other side was never saying much and listening a great deal. Fleming led the quite life of senior research worker and family man. In 1921, he took a cottage at Barton Mills in Suffolk. He could relax their and renew the pleasures of his Ayrshire youth. In 1924, he got the son and named as Robert.

Fleming once suffered from heavy colds and catarrhs. He began his bacteriological investigations. He cultivated a drop from his nose in appropriate medium and found after three days strange large micro organisms in the medium. In the course of future experiments, he added a little diluted mucus from his nose to the culture medium. To his surprise, he noticed that strange micro organisms were disappeared. He could thus prove that body's defence mechanism can produce the substances which are able to combat the micro organisms causing diseases. He found that human tears were particularly rich in such substances. This substance is referred as 'Lysozyme'. It is derived from Greek words for solution and fermentation. Fleming regarded some of his work on lysozyme as, without exception, the best he ever did. Lysozyme is now established as natural antiseptic present in tears, mucus, Saliva, pus, blood serum egg albumen in plants also.

Fleming became Assistant Director of Wright's Department and in 1928 he also became University professor in Bacteriology. Fleming was a good but not brilliant lecturer. His strong points as a teacher were his friendliness and helping nature. Late in 1928, he was examining staphylococcus cultures under the microscope. During this series of observations he discovered that the mould which forms the blue feathery fungus on cheese or jam can be destroy staphylococci. He further found that the fluid in which the mould grew could stop the growth of staphylococci even when diluted to 1 part in 1000! He attributed this powerful action to the presence of a substance called – 'PENICILLIN'. He noticed that, unlike carbolic acid, the penicillin preparation did not harm the white corpuscles. This biological substance was of a kind with which his imagination had been preoccupied for years. It was able to destroy dangerous bacteria without interfering with the body's natural protective system. He found that it has effective against the micro-organisms of pneumonia, diphtheria and veneral diseases. So also on those which cause sore throats and boils. It was indeed the great discovery. Fleming's expertise was not sufficient to isolate and purify penicillin as he was not a chemist but bacteriologist. He published his discovery in 1929.

In 1928, in connection with investigations of the mechanism of immunity; Florey undertook study of lysozyme. He further succeeded in preparing pure and crystalline specimens of lysozyme. Florey and Chain later on also studied penicillin, and could prepare fairly unbelievable power of killing dangerous germs, even when diluted to one part in many millions. They showed that it was very effective against blood poisoning in mice. It was then tested on human patient. A policeman in an Oxford hospital was dying from blood poisoning. Existing treatments offered no hope of his survival, so the purified penicillin was tried. It produced an immediate and great improvement in his condition. But the small amount of penicillin could not save his life. The policeman after his remarkable rally relapsed and died.

In August 1942, a patient in St. Mary's Hospital, who was one of Fleming's friend, was dying from streptococcal meningitis. His name was Harry Lambert. Fleming telephoned Florey and asked him to spare some of the very precious penicillin. Florey's response was swift. He had given Fleming all the penicillin they had in Oxford. Fleming began series of experiments, ultimately injecting doses directly into his friend's spine on August 6, 1942 evening. It was an historic occasion; it was the moment when the man who discovered penicillin—the miracle drug which transformed medical history for all time—first injected it into a patient, and saw its incredible power working before his own eyes. Within a few days the patient's temperature became normal and he was able to get up before the end of month. The cure was almost miraculous. Though penicillin was discovered in September 1928, Journalists heard the case of Harvy Lambert in the summer of 1942 more intensely and with wide applause. Next days were the days of penicillin hitting the newspaper headlines. In 1945, Alexander Fleming, for his discovery of penicillin, shared the Nobel Prize for medicine with two scientists who headed the Oxford team that gave penicillin to the World—Howard Florey and Ernst Chain.

Fleming's discovery was accidental. He reacted 'There are thousands of different moulds and there are thousands of different bacteria and that chance put that mould in the right spot and at the right time was like winning the Irish sweep'. It would not have possible if Fleming would not have been painstakingly observant. His further remarks are worth practicing 'All of us, in our ordinary pursuits, can do research, by continual and critical observation. If something unusual happens we should think about it and try to find out what it means... There can be little doubt that the future of humanity depends greatly on the freedom of researcher to pursue his own line of thought. It is not an unreasonable ambition in a research worker that he should become famous, but the man who undertakes research with the ultimate aim of wealth or power is in the wrong place'. Alec's discovery of penicillin and lysozyme are examples of chance happenings superbly turned to scientific riches. Pasteur once said, 'In the field of experimentation chance favours the prepared mind' which had dominating role.

Fleming published his paper related to lysozyme in Royal Society of London's publication. The paper was entitled—on a Remarkable Bacteriolytic Element found in Tissues and secretions'. He could get partial success in its isolation in pure form. He could do qualitative work and not quantitative one. Slowly he became expert and in 1945 he told 'I play with microbes. There are of course many rules in this play—but when you have acquired knowledge and experience it is very pleasant to break the rules and to be able to find something that nobody had thought of...'.

Honours showered down on the shy and sensitive Alexander Fleming. In July 1944, he was knighted in the basement of Buckingham Palace. He was proud to receive in the same year the Freedom of Paddington where he had spent all his medical life (St. Mary's Hospital). He also received the Freedom of Darvel, the small Scottish town where he had between at school. He had refused to patent penicillin. If he would have patented penicillin, he could have earned millions of pounds as royalty. He was elected a Fellow of the Royal Society in 1943. After the death of Wright in 1947, he succeeded him as a Director of the Inoculation Department at St. Mary's Hospital. This was subsequently reconstituted as the Wright-Fleming Institute of microbiology.

Fleming received the Moxon Medal from the Royal College of Physicians, the Cameron Prize of the University of Edinburgh, the Gold Medal of the Royal Society of Medicine, and medical and scientific honours from societies in many countries. As many as thirty universities from America and Europe conferred on him honorary doctorates. He particularly valued the medal he received personally from the Pope, and his membership of the Pontifical Academy of Sciences. He received all of these with unaffected modesty. He was particularly pleased with letters and appreciation from humble people such as a collection of signatures from a group of workmen or a letter from a child or from some poor person who had benefited from penicillin treatment.

He presented his youthful energy and enthusiasm. He retained his lean and muscular figure, his neat clothes and his bow tie. He had a very wide range of human interests.

Sareen's illness was a problem during his glorious years. He had been devoted to her she had given him support he so badly needed. She died on October 28, 1949. They had 34 years of married happy and contented life. Fleming was heart broken. He used to sit in a room whose doors were always shut. He could continue his research day and night. He married a young Greek Bacteriologist Dr. Amalia Voureka in 1953. She was a brilliant Biologist who had received a British Council bursary to work in England. She was in Fleming's laboratory from 1946. Their happiness was shortlived. Alec died very suddenly on March 11, 1955 of heart attack (coronary thrombosis). That was the disease which his drug was powerless to control. He was busy in research till his end. He was planning for the problem of natural immunity. The end, however was very swift. His wife was with him when he died. He was buried in St Paul's Cathedral.

The discovery of penicillin has revolutionized the treatment of disease. Penicillin and the whole group of 'antibiotics' it triggered on, have miraculous impact on the medical field. Fleming, a brilliant research worker did not confine himself to observing with new angle, but more importantly he took action at once'.

He was elected reactor of Edinburgh University in 1952. It was award in his native Scotland which gave him particular pleasure. That was the place where he said, "I gained much general knowledge and when I went to medical school I had a great advantage over my fellow students who were straight from school and had never got away from their books into the school of life". One should ever remember this brilliant student from the school of life!

16

Linus Pauling

Linus Pauling is the unique name who got two Nobel Prizes unshared, for his outstanding contributions in two altogether different fields. He got the Nobel Prize in Chemistry in 1954 and that in Peace in 1962. Pauling was a person with extraordinary talent and intuition, great confidence and courage; excellent in arguments and vehemence. Pauling was a phenomenon in Chemistry. He had wide spectrum of contributions in the fields of physics, quantum mechanics, physical chemistry, theoretical organic chemistry, biochemistry, biology and medical chemistry. He had deep insight in both the aspects namely theoretical and practical of the subject. Therefore his work is quite impressive. Pauling was also subject to considerable criticism by some scientists for his unusual methods and approximations. He was accused of mathematical deficiency and lack of thoroughness.

Pauling was married to Ava Helen Miller in 1923. They met in chemistry class. It is interesting to note that when they both took an intelligence test she scored higher than he did. He warned her honestly 'If I had to choose between you and science, I am not sure what I would choose you'. Pauling was always somewhat detached in human relationship. Ava Helen gradually educated Pauling in politics and society. It was her ideas and influence that led him to take the radical positions on political questions that occupied much of his later life. Besides sheer knowledge, status, prestige and money were important to Pauling. He was the most practical and little self centred. He had a good conceit of himself and to the end of his life although he had many honours and prizes, he used to point out that it was he who had discovered this or what. Pauling was exceptionally good in finding out correct answer to the problem. If corrupt answer is not sought out, at least his guess can lend to minimum number of possible answers in which one is certain to get exact answer. To get new ideas you have to have facts and information about existing ideas to the fullest extent. Pauling had an excellent memory and quickly could acquire a huge stock of facts, especially about chemistry. Pauling was however the master of structural chemistry. Pauling had a long and consistent happy married life till his wife died in 1981. They had three sons and a daughter.

Linus Pauling was born in Portland in Oregon State on 28th February 1901. His father was pharmacist. They had a medical shop and the specialty was one can get popular medicine which can purify the blood. Pauling lost his father when he was still in school. The family had to face poverty and adversity. This gave Pauling the real experience of life and the habit of fighting and faces the situation boldly and with confidence. As a child, Pauling was interested in insects and minerals. He used to work in his spare time to earn and support family. He finished his school but he could not receive the diploma since he did not complete the course in civics because of his family background that time. The school awarded the diploma after he received the Nobel Prize for peace. He then joined Oregon Agricultural College at Corvallis as an undergraduate student after completing the requirements. His consummate faith in his own intellect and boldness was evident even at that time. On one occasion in which the Dean was addressing to the student assembly, Pauling interfered and corrected some of the Dean's statements. He did this with positive view in order to avoid misinformation to large number of students. Dean also took it graciously. There was break in his undergraduate studies after two years because of financial problems. He was then made an assistant to teach quantitative analysis and could continue his studies. In Fred Allen he could have good teacher in chemistry. There were few others. He got B.S. degree in 1922 in chemical engineering. By this time he had read the papers of Langmuir and Lewis about atoms and molecules. Lewis had on him profound influence. He had dedicated his classical book 'The Nature of The Chemical Bond' to G.N. Lewis in 1938. He had taken mathematics, physics and crystallography courses in undergraduate studies. Ava Helen was his close friend in those days. They got married and it is reported earlier.

There was considerable pressure on him to take up a job to support his family but he decided to pursue post graduate studies. His obvious choice was University of California, Berkeley where G.N. Lewis was presiding the famous department. The alternative choice was California Institute of Technology (CALTECH) where Prof. Noyes was the chairman of the department and Robert Millikan was the president. He got the admission first to Caltech and he joined Caltech.

In Caltech, as per Noyes's advice he joined his Ph. D. studies in crystallography under the guidance of R. Dickinson. He studied the structures of several minerals. Peter Debye visited Caltech during his Ph. D. days and he wrote a paper with him also. He took Ph. D. in 1925. Noyes wanted him to go to Europe for further studies and he helped him to get the fellowship. He studied quantum mechanics in Europe, most of the time he was in the Arnold Sommerfeld's Institute for theoretical physics at Munich. He also worked with Bohr at Copenhagen and with Schrodinger in Zurich for some time. During his stay with Sommerfeld he also came in contact with Heitler and London. He wrote classic paper on the properties of multi electron atoms at revealed by quantum mechanics. He tried to correlate the atomic properties predicted by quantum mechanics and that from study of crystallography. Lawrence Bragg, one of the great scientists that time did not particularly appreciated Pauling views. Bragg was authority in X-Ray diffraction. Pauling could thus get wide range of contacts with great people in Europe.

Pauling joined Caltech in 1927 as an assistant professor in theoretical chemistry. He worked as associate professor during 1929 to 31 and full professor during 1931 to 34. He had a long innings with Caltech up to 1963. He reconciled the Bohr model of atom with Lewis model of atoms and molecules. He described valence bond approach and resonance, ionicity, hybridisation etc. These are now basic concepts in chemical bonding.

In 1930, he initiated research on electron diffraction of gases and derived the structures of many important molecules of great relevance to the understanding of chemical bonding. He also investigated other topics like electro negativity and hydrogen bonding. He also published his work extensively and with authenticity and certainty. His work was biblical reference for chemistry. David Harker, Linus Pauling's one time student and protein crystallographer; asked Pauling how he got such large number of good ideas. Pauling replied that he used to take all his ideas and threw away the bad ones. Pauling's life was characterized by the way he handled his good ideas but perhaps he did not throw away quite enough and got criticised. Pauling was fountain of knowledge that changed the direction of chemistry.

In 1935, he wrote the classic book entitled 'Introduction of Quantum Mechanics and Applications to Chemistry' along with Wilson. In 1938 Pauling wrote the immortal book 'Nature of Chemical Bond' Pauling worked extensively. He got Nobel Prize in 1954 for his work in chemistry. Some people think he got the Prize little late.

He then shifted the focus of his work to biology. He experimontod with haemoglobin, proteins, polypeptides, amino acids etc, He also studied denaturation of proteins, irreversible change in the structure and properties of proteins due to heat or chemical treatment. e.g. egg when boiled this change occurs. Dorothy Wrinch was working on the structure of proteins and proposed cyclic or ring model for their structures. Pauling proved it to be wrong and proposed linkage of amino acids to form peptide bond repeatedly to get polypeptides and proteins. By 1950 Pauling and Corey worked out the alpha helical coiled structure of proteins. Pauling used to express himself with a pinch of bitterness about others and it was annoying, many scientists resented his approach towards dealing the people.

In 1949, he wrote the famous paper on sickle cell anaemia. Cells change their shape and get the shape of Crescent. This is due to change in molecular structure and therefore disease was referred as 'molecular disease'. By electrophoresis experiment he could prove that these deformed cells and normal cells have different speed during electrophoresis. He also studied the properties of haemoglobin, the important constituent of red blood cells and its interactions with oxygen and carbon monoxide. He could judge the nature of physical flaw of haemoglobin in sickle cell anaemia. This revolutionised the medical field.

He also studied that if some micro organisms bacteria, viruses or fungi enter the human body (or the poisonous substances or harmful substances) there is natural mechanism that produces antibodies to fight against. These are immunological problems. The chemicals which are used as anesthetics change temporarily the molecular structures in the body. He studied the structural effects of anesthetics and body chemicals. He could well illustrate various important phenomenons in medical biochemistry and heredity. He founded the branch 'Orthomolecular Medicine'. It includes preservation of health by manipulating the concentration of substances normally present in the body. He realized the cause of mental disease/disorders on molecular structure basis.

His most debatable and disputable research was about Vitamin C (ascorbic acid). It was the big controversy in medical field. He was however extensively studied the subject taking into consideration all its aspects and could prove its effectiveness on common cold, flu, cancer and AIDS even. He published many papers and wrote books 'Vitamin C and common cold' (1970), Vitamin C and flu (1976), Cancer and VC (Vitamin C) (1979) and How to live longer and feel better (1986). He also published his results about the use of Vitamin C on AIDS (1990). He himself was used for his experimentations about Vitamin C. He was suffering from cancer and he used to consume daily eighteen grams of Vitamin C through recommended or tolerable dose of Vitamin C is 60 milligrams. This is what Megavitamin Therapy'. In his medical research especially about cancer he was in full coordination with Scottish Physician Ewan Cameron. He also started research on orthomolecular psychiatry and shoed that mental patients were deficient in ascorbic acid (vitamin C), pyridoxime (Vitamin B_6) and pantothenic acid (Vitamin B_3). Thus Pauling worked for well being and health of human race.

Pauling's work in the scientific field is discussed above. He was quite close to solving structure of DNA (Deoxyribonucleic Acid), the wonder molecule responsible for heredity. The credit of DNA's structure (á alpha helix model) goes to Watson and Crick who shared the Nobel Prize for the purpose. Pauling met Einstein with whom he had discussions on human rights, determinism, peace and other topics. His wife was also active about 'peace'. In 1950 Pauling made a public statement on the need to avoid war. He made fervent appeals for stopping nuclear testing and warned the world community about dangers of nuclear radiations. Pauling wrote to President Eisenhower pointing the danger of nuclear weapons particularly it's biological effects. He wrote the book 'No More War (1958)', the copy of the book was also sent to the president, He stated 'may our great nation United States if America' be the leader in bringing morality into 'its proper place of primary importance in the conduct of world affairs'. He was not received properly and there was tremendous antagonism towards him. Pauling called nuclear testing, a crime against humanity. In 1958, January, he and his wife appealed American Government by presenting petition signed by 11021 scientists about the ban of nuclear testing. He also appealed to United Nations. US senate was much disturbed over this. Public opinion became quite against him. At Caltech pressures were increasing to cut him short, he had to resign from the chairmanship of the chemistry division in 1958. Many universities stopped calling him for lectures as he was slowly considered antinational or anti American. In 1962 Pauling was leading a picket line in front of the white house. The same evening there was a dinner for the American Nobel Laureates hosted by President Kennedy. He was publicly accused as a communist sympathizer. In 1962 Linus Pauling received the Nobel Prize for peace.

This created more problems for him. The chemists at Caltech did not celebrate his second Nobel Prize. Journalists and newspapers considered it as an insult to

America or slapping in the face. Pauling was harassed for this peace activity right from 1954. He also resigned from membership of American Chemical Society. Pauling did not have proper place to work. He worked during 1963-67 at the centre for the study of Democratic Institutions in Santa Barbara, University of California (1967-69) and Stanford University (1969-74) . He founded the Linus Pauling Institute of Science and Medicine in 1974.

The days slowly changed in Linus's favour. In 1970 his name was eliminated from the list of persons considered to be communist sympathizers. By 1975, the US administrators seem to have fully exonerated Pauling. He was awarded National Medal of Science in 1975. In 1976, the American Chemical Society celebrated its centenary. He was asked to give ACS centenary lecture. Everybody was quite happy to receive and honour him. In 1991, on his 90th birthday, the US National Academy of sciences honoured him with a special citation. He was the member of American National Academy of Science, Royal Society London, Russian Academy of sciences and many others. He received Davy Medal of Royal Society (1940), Phillips Memorial Award from American College Of Physicians (1956), Avogadro's Medal of Italian Academy of Sciences (1956), International Lenin Peace Prize (1968-69) and Gandhi Peace Prize. He was honoured by many universities by conferring on him their doctorates degrees. He was the person who stood by the things he believed irrespective of anything. He had to undergo personal suffering and harassment for long period. He also suffered physically by cancer and died on 19th August 1994.

Pauling was wizard of enormous energy. He was ahead of his times. His life span has covered almost twentieth century. Even in his late ages he worked with new ideas like quasi-crystals (1985) and superconductivity (1988). These works were as novel and fresh that of his prime age work in structure and bonding. He kept on working even when he was awfully suffering from cancer and experimented on self. His work will definitely impact not only on twentyfirst century science but also on science of all time especially chemistry!!

17

Herman Mark

Herman Mark is now looked upon as 'Founding Father of Polymer Field'. It is a comparatively recent but very fast growing field. If one looks around the food we eat, the cloths we wear, rubber and plastic articles that we use, they are all nothing but polymers. It is versatile and ever expanding field. Though the originator of the idea of polymer is the German Chemist H. Staudinger, H. Mark with his patient working and varied approach put the field on firm foundations. Polymers are large molecules (macromolecules) formed by joining simple small molecules repeatedly by covalent bonds. They are put to variety of uses and their properties can be 'tailor made' as per our requirements. They are available in different forms, colours, strength and can be blended with other materials. Plastics, rubbers and fibres are three important forms of polymers. The examples of polymers include Polyethylene, Poly Vinyl Chloride (PVC), Nylon, Terylene, Teflon, Epoxy Resins, Bakelite, Melamine Polyurethanes (used for rigid and flexible foams and high resistant rubbers) etc.

H. Mark led a long and busy life of about 97 years. He wrote his autobiography titled : *'My life—One Hundred Years of Random Walk'.* Recently in a series of books one chemist, he was also contributed one volume titled—*'From Small Organic Molecules to Large'* [Profiles, Pathways and Dreams J.I. Seeman Series Editor (1993)]. He puts his life as "I am being travelled. It is a form of Brownian Motion". Brownian motion is fast spontaneous random motion of particles that are colloidal in nature (macro molecular). He was born in Vienna (1895). He had strong attachment to his place of birth. He was a highly decorated officer in Austrian Army in the World War I. He was wounded there severely during the war but fortunately could survive. He had 15 medals to his credit. One very important medal was for 'Disobeying orders of retreat'. He had to keep away in war for 5 years. His contribution in Italy- Austria war is remarkable.

He then took his Ph.D.(1921) under Dr. Slenk and started working as an instructor in Berlin, then at Dahlem (Kaiser Wilhelm Institute) and Ludwigshafen (I.G. Farben Co.) – all in Germany. He had to leave Germany due to Nazi's trouble (brief and horrifying experiences and even imprisonment) for Canada and finally settled in United States at Poly-technique Institute of Brooklyn, New York.

Mark's accomplishments varied and fascinating. They include :

1. Applying modern Physics and Chemistry. Multidisciplinary approach especially in the field of fast electron diffractions.
2. Synthesis, characterisation, properties and reactivates of natural and synthetic polymers.
3. Propagation of polymer science by making it as the part of curricula. The first step in this way was taken in the University of Vienna as long back as 1932.
4. He turned every corner to nourish the field of polymer science. He was a prolific writer and an excellent lecturer. His style of lecturing was slow, careful and pleasing. His lectures were so planned and perfect that they

could have been printed just as they were given. He was the key person to start the 'Journey of Polymer Science' and 'Journal of Applied Polymer Science'. He has written more than 600 articles and about 20 books! He was instrumental in preparing Encyclopaedia of Chemical Technology. 'Chemistry in life' was interesting and popular programme given by him on TV. He thus could gain the title 'founding father' of polymer field.

Mark as human being was very polite, kept good relations with everybody—family members, friends, students, relatives and foes as well. He had perfectly cordial family life. He married Marie (Mimi) Schramek in 1922. His hospitality is experienced by many great people from the world. He had eye for fun and loved celebrations especially birthday parties. His 85th birthday was celebrated at number of places and had remarked "My birthday starts in April and ends in October" He was quite optimistic. He was a nice blend of discipline and freedom. He loved music. He could play violin and piano. He liked to witness plays. However, he did not like to grade students. He used to do that job mechanically—2 A's followed by 1 B was his repeating cycle of grading. Once one student who was very good was graded as 'B' in his cycle, when the student questioned his grade Herman Mark advised him to re appear in a fashion so that he could get A. He was influenced by his teacher Dr. Hlawaty. He therefore chose science as his career and took interest in Physics and Mathematics. Other personalities who had strong impact include Emit Fischer-Berlin (Chemist), Albert Einstein—Prague (Mathematician and Philosopher), Ernest Rutherford—England (Physicist) and Mark Curie—Poland during their visit to Vienna.

It is worth noting the differences between H. Staudinger and H. Mark. Staudinger reflected genius, egoistic and self centred personality whereas Mark reflected a polite, open-minded and human spirit. One has remarked about Mark's greatness as 'He does not seem bitter, yet he has a right to be'. Staudinger did not have high opinion about Mark. Staudinger sent back the gift sent by Mark with remark 'Unopened'. The books written by Mark were treated by Staudinger as 'Not science but propaganda'. Irrespective of these facts Staudinger was received by Mark with full heart and warm welcome in the States. This was also a surprise to Staudinger.

It was difficult to sell the concept of polymer or large molecules to the scientific world Staudinger and Mark both worked in the field in their own ways and finally succeeded. It was difficult job as the great scientists of the type 'Emil Fischer and Wieland P Karver, Nobel Laureates' were against it. Polymer concept was believed to be incredible unnecessary and even impossible. In 1920's Staudinger used to emphasise his concept based on solution viscosities and assumed rigid rod like structure for polymer molecules. Polymer solution therefore behaves as viscous and does not flow easily. Mark used 'flexible-structure' based on modern X-ray studies. What worked well was the combination of the work of both of them. Two instances are worth quoting here. In one discussion the comment came "Suppose you are Zoologist and make an expedition to Central Africa. After your return you give a lecture and say "In the plains and steppers of the Congo, I have seen elephants that are 80 meters long and 20 meters high" with long range snap shots. Nobody will believe" Staudinger's arguments were based on 'long range snap shots, where Herman Marks on actual measurements (X-Rays) and more reliable' In Faraday society meeting in Cambridge in 1935, other instances occurred. Staudinger used to have match stocks about 10-20 inches long to demonstrate polymer molecules. These match stocks are still preserved in Munich. He was explaining in the meeting : "These match shocks represent macro molecules in solution and are responsible for high viscocities of these systems. Then he broke one and added "If molecules are degraded, their strength is reduced and the viscosity drops dramatically" Staudinger referred to the Chairman E.E. Rideal and asked "Is it clear?" Rideal saw the broken stocks and said: 'Yes. I think it is perfectly clear but wrong'.

Mark's X-ray works on fibrous macromolecular substances begin in 1935. He studied cellulose and proved that natural rubber was 'cis'polymer and not 'trans' polymer as proposed by Staudinger 'Cis' and 'trans' are isomeric molecules with same molecular formulae but different structural formulae. These structures differ in geometrical arrangement about a carbon – carbon double bond. Same side arrangement is 'Cis' and opposite aside arrangement is 'trans'. Mark also studied earlier element like Zink (Zn), Tin (Sn) and Carbon (C) and compounds like Ammonia (NH_3), Methane (CH_4) and Borane (BH_3). On Prof. Meyers' recommendation, Mark shifted to Ludwigshafen (I.G. Farben Co.) and along with electron diffraction he used spectroscopic—optical and infra red methods for studies. At I.G. Farben he developed solution spinning technique for cellulose acetates. These polymers were good in strength and in lustre similar to silk. These are rayons. In mid 1930's he prepared copolymers from butadiene and styrene and from butadiene and acrylonitrile, copolymers are obtained from two starting compounds. Starting these proved to be most important synthetic rubber. He could develop also polystyrene (PS), one of the popular plastics today. It is referred as Thermo-Cole used for decorative purposes, moulding and extrusion. This polymer is obtained from the basic compound styrene which is the monomer of this product.

In summer of 1932, Hitler took over and as Mark's father was a Jew, he was treated as a foreigner. He suffered many human, political and scientific indignities in those days. Then he moved to Vienna and studied condensation polymerization. He also took mountaineering and climbing expeditions, to collect heavy water from glaciers. He thus had altogether different experiences.

He then shifted to Canada (1938-40) to work with Canadian International Pulp and Paper Co. and then to Brooklyn (USA). At Brooklyn he studied for shellac substitutes. Shellac was imported in states from India and Indonesia. During war period he was involved in developing armed snow mobile—'Weasal'. For the purpose he extensively studied properties of snow and ice. Then he worked on iceberg which could be used as 'floating landing strip' This was achieved by incorporating wood pulp and even saw dust in iceberg. Alfrey's contribution in this regard as supervisor was very important. He was also involved in landing craft 'Duke'. He was consultant to 'NASA'.

He was one of the key person in developing Weizmann Institute Palestine (1946). He visited many places (100) in the world. He had often travelled between Europe and America (500 times). He had interacted with about 1000 scientists and engineers. His work with cellulose gave him leadership of WIP for whole tree technology for energy production. Separation of cellulose from pulping of tropical wood species remained his major interest. He took many patents and was involved in many litigations as an expert in the field of a polymers. One important hobby was related to instant photography developed by Edwin Land. He used a chain of paper clips to demonstrate how polymer molecules behave. He appeared 60 times in court as an expert witness in 40 years and won because of his planned, steady arguments and convincing approach. He reacted at his 80th birthday. "How is it that in spite of all, something worth while came out of it." The answer to this was his honest hard work in his undertakings irrespective of the nature and type of the work. Whenever Mark left the places, his colleagues found "Mark left a well ordered and orderly house" for their pursuits.

He got many awards and honours. He could not get the Nobel Prize. It was awarded to H. Staudinger (1953). He could get National Medal of Science from President Jimmy Carter in 1980. He reacted to this by saying "Polymer Science was now in main stream of Chemistry" This reflects his approach towards 'work' and not the outcome of work or rewards out of work' He was nourished right from his school days (1906-1909) by Greek and Latin thinking. He was especially impressed by lecture of Karl Prinz, Kanlian Philosopher. 'Truth, dependability, benevolence and the absence of analice' were the four pillars of Mark's existence. He followed a rule—'Keep, cool and never lose your composure'. He died on 6th April 1992. This great scientist will ever be remembered for his work as a propagator of polymer science and his composure.

18

Richard Feynman

Richard Feynman received the Nobel Prize in 1965 shared with Julian Schwinger an American and Sin-Itiro Tomonaga a Japanese physicists. His immediate reaction when he first learnt that he received the prize was as follows in his own words.

"Someone called me at 3.30 to 4.00 in the morning.

'Professor Feynman?'

'Hey! Why are you bothering me at this time in the morning?'

'I thought you would like to know that you've won the Nobel Prize'.

'Yeah, but I am sleeping! It would have been better if you had called me in the morning'— and I hang up".

His life is therefore quite fascinating and in many respects all together different than rest of the people in the field of research and teaching. Ralph Leighton has rightly said, "One person could invest so much innocent mischief in one life is surely an inspiration!" Feynman had an extraordinary capacity to solve the problems. He was characterized by provocative, mischievousness, indignant impatience with pretension and hypocrisy. In him 'mischief' was highly personified with brilliance and innovativeness. At the age of 17 to 18 years, in one summer he was working in the hotel that was ran by his aunt. There also he worked with full involvement and tried to follow different route than the rest. He had an experience—'I learnt there that innovation is a very difficult thing in real world' His nature did-not allow him to keep away from creativity. He remained always enterprising in inventing ideas and playing with them. His life is full of such experiences and to know these in really thrilling and motivating. One really gets stuck to know about him more and more.

He quite reluctantly went to receive the Nobel Prize. There also he behaved differently than the set traditions. After he got the prize he was invited to talk in front of all types of audience. He could avoid many occasions but some of the places he had to go for some reason or the other. He found it quite ridiculous. His one experience is worth quoting. He went to Rio at the invitation of Brazil government. There were huge carnival celebrations. He was received with loud applause. Samba schools were playing rhythmic music. There was also playing on drums and cow bells. Feynman himself was good in music and he could appreciate the spirit with which he was received. The invitation was with the initiative of minister of tourism. For those carnivals famous actress Gina Lollobrigida was invited. She could not come and Feynman was replaced in her place by that minister as the timely arrangement. Of course, the minister lost his position in the government because of this. Feynman enjoyed all that situation with no bitterness or malice for anybody. He took it as a fun. It requires a broad perspective of mind which he had much. He had unique mixture of high intelligence, unquenchable curiosity and eternal scepticism. He was dominating during the conversations with his friends and students. He was received with all greetings by any type of audience and people.

Feynman was born on May 11, 1918 in a small town for Rockaway on the outskirt of New York. He stayed there for 17 years. At the age of 11 to 12 years he set laboratory in his house. He kept experimenting with different instruments and sets—radios. He could repair things which other could not do. He became popular as—'he can set up radios by thinking' He was genius. He then studied for his B.S. degree from 1935-39 at prestigious MIT Massachusetts. During 1939 to 43 he was at Princeton University. He completed there his Ph. D. He was then at Los Alamos up to 1946. In that place United States Atomic Bomb Project—'Manhattan Project' was going on with all seriousness and meticulous planning in a laboratory. He got married with Arlene in 1941. He was staying at Albuquerque where his wife was suffering from TB. He had to make frequent visits between Albuquerque and Los Alamos. Unfortunately his wife died in 1946. He then joined University of Cornell Ithaca. He was there from 1946 to 1951. He visited Brazil twice on 1949 to 1951. He also visited Japan in 1951. He then joined another prestigious institute—Caltech from America. He was there since 1951. He got married for the second time with Mary Lou (1953). It could also not last long. He married for the third time with English lady named Gweneth.

Feynman was peculiar man. Many funny instants can be quoted from his life. The language has its peculiar intonation. It can vary from person to person or place to place. Intonation also depends upon whether it is your mother tongue or whether you have mastered it after learning. Feynman had trick nack of genuine imitation of various intonations. He went as a father of a sister and sang a song in tone. It was neither Italian nor Latin. It was in a tone required, people interpreted it in the way they liked and appreciated. He used to have many coloured dreams. It could be with many people but he used to seriously interpret and they used to be funny often. He accepted many unbelievable bets and could win many. He ate a six tablets and three bottles of Coca-Cola in any sequence. The Coca-Cola and aspirin together was thought to be poisonous and nobody would try it.

During his Los Alamos days, the things that were worked there, were quite confidential and all used to keep their reports in a safe. Feynman used to open those safes and people used to be under high tension. He was very mischievous safe cracker. He used to remember the last two numbers and feel the snatches by trial and error. He could do it with ease and intelligence. There were number of fighting instances in men's room due to his nature. One such took place in Buffalo. They could be due to misunderstanding or hot debates or pun. In a hotel he enquired about champagne, answer was

'Sir, that's sixteen dollars a bottle'—Waiter.

'NEVER MIND'—Feynman.

He thought 'Never Mind' the price when I (Feynman) meant 'Never Mind ' the Champagne.

Las Vegas is a place in America quite popular for gambling and casino, hotels and food. He used to enjoy the life of Las Vegas in a very natural style as if he was the resident of Las Vegas and not a visitor. Feynman was good in drawing the portraits. He learned and mastered that art from his friend Jirayr Zorthian (Jerry). He started with nothing and in a due course he became expert. He was thus quick learner in any field. Many of his portraits were kept in Bullock's (Big Departmental stores at Pasadena). There were also many interesting experiences in this field. He prepared some drawing for the massage parlour. It was not accepted there for some reason or the other. The drawing was very good and it suited to the test of one office. He remarked 'So the massage parlour drawing ended up in the office of weather forecaster.'

Feynman was an effective communicator. He was a popular teacher. One of the instances with stenographer is very illustrious. He said, 'you see I'm a steno typist, and I type everything that is said here. Now, when the other fellows talk I type what they say, but I don't understand what they are saying. But every time you get up to ask a question or to say something. I understand exactly what you mean—what the question is and what you are saying—so I thought you can't be a professor!!"

'The Feynman lectures on Physics' which are published in three volumes by Addison-Wisley publishing company, Inc. is in conformity with his immortality as a teacher. These lectures were given at Caltech. 180 students were tried. He used to meet them two times a week along with teaching assistants for a group of 15 to 20 students. There used to be laboratory session once in a week. The first volume of his lectures has 52 chapters, second 41 chapters and third 21 chapters. Matthew Sandy from Stanford University wrote 'Now, he has given two years of his ability and his energy to his lectures on physics for beginning students. For them he has distilled the essence of his knowledge, and has created in terms they can hope to grasp a picture of the physicist's Universe. To his lectures he has brought the brilliance and clarity of his thought, the originality and vitality of his approach, and contagious enthusiasm of his delivery.

It was a joy to behold "Though these books he has widely spread the contagious joy of physics to thousands and thousands of students all over the world. 'The story of physics one finds in these books would not have been, except for the extraordinary ability and industry of Richard P. Feynman.' is one of the noteworthy comments. Feynman has his comments about his approach—'finally, may I add that the main purpose of my teaching has not been to prepare you for some examination—it was not even to prepare you to serve industry or the military. I wanted most to give you some appreciation of the wonderful world and the physicist's way of looking at it, which I believe is a major part of the true culture of modern times'. His views about education are also very important to practice by the all in this field—'I think, however, that there isn't any solution to this problem of education other than to realize that the best teaching can be done only when there is a direct individual relationship between a student and a good teacher—a situation in which the student discusses the ideas, thinks about the things and talks about the things. It's impossible to learn very much by simple sitting in a lecture or even by simply doing problems that are assigned, But in our modern times we have so many students to teach that we have to try to find some substitute for the ideal. Perhaps my lectures can make some contribution. Perhaps in some small place where there are individual teachers and students, they may get some inspiration or some ideas from the lectures. Perhaps they will or some ideas from the lectures. Perhaps they will have fun thinking them through or going on to develop some of the ideas further'. His hopes are materialised and will also be in future!

He liked openness in the system and new approach. He had two cyclotrons for his experiences. One with MIT was neat, clean and gold plated. The other with Princeton was open and untidy. "It reminded me of my laboratory at home. I suddenly realized why Princeton was getting results. They were working with the instruments. They built the instrument, they knew where everything was, they knew now everything worked there was no engineer involved except may be he was working there too! It was much smaller than the cyclotron at MIT. It was wonderful! Because they worked with it"—It reflects his approach towards the things. The second experience was to start working and get engrossed in a problem in mathematics and/ or topology—"Then I come along and by differentiating under the integral sign and often it worked, so I got a great reputation for doing integrals, only because my box of tools was different from everybody else's and they had tried all their tools on it before giving the problem to me." He could solve the problem with new approach.

Feynman was a genius. Hans Bethe has said—"There are two types of genius. Ordinary geniuses do great things, but they leave you room to believe that you could do the same if only you worked hard enough. Then there are magicians and you can have no idea how they do it. Feynman was a magician". It is reflected in the fact as he made is Nobel winning discovery in a hotel. He said "I went on to work out equations of Wobbles. Then I thought about how electron orbits start to more in relativity. Then there is the Dirac equation in electrodynamics. And then quantum electrodynamics.. I was playing.. It was effortless. It was like uncorking a bottle. Everything flowed out effortlessly. The diagrams and the whole business that I got the Nobel Prize for, came from the piddling ground with the wobbling plate" The incidence was 'the plate was thrown and wobbled in a hotel'. Red medallation of Carnell on the plate was going around. He observed that medallation went around faster than wobbling. The trail of thoughts moved in his mind and he worked out equations. He believed that experience of nature is important. He would start by defining science as an understanding of the behaviour of nature. He could also give philosophical talks about science on the other side he could crack the jokes and do lot many mischief. It was unique

'Versatility'. He tried to evolve theory of liquid helium—now laws of quantum dynamics explain the strange phenomenon of super fluidity. In 1950, he correlated properties of liquid helium as microscopically observable quantum behaviour. During his study Feynman proposed and later confirmed 'particle' of energy called vortex excitation. In 1957, Feynman with Murray Gell-Mann proposed current theory of weak interactions among subatomic particles. Such interactions are among are responsible for spontaneous radioactivity. Their theory explained 'weak' magnetism observed in radioactive decay of nuclei. In 1960, he proposed 'quark'—most fundamental entity.

His Nobel Prize was for developing theory; Relativistic quantum electrodynamics. It was worked out in 1940 and published in 1948. It deals with the interaction of electromagnetic radiation with charged subatomic particles. He also invented a diagrammatic calculatory technique known as—Feynman diagram. During the early stages of the Manhattan project, he also worked on U235/U238 isotope separately. He also worked on the laws of beta delays. Two particles 'Tau' and 'Theta' with same mass were studied. One disintegrates into two 'Pions' and the other in three 'Pions'. They have same half life. He had some experience as a chemist. It was about electroplating plastics. It is still a challenging field. He had also worked in biological field—m-RNA (messenger – ribonucleic acid) which has a role in protein synthesis. He had also an opportunity to work with Watson who along with Crick gave current structure of DNA molecule. In short he had quite varied experience in the research field and had his own impact.

He used to ridicule many bad particles in America. He noticed that giving bribes and taking bribes was common. He was appointed in a committee to recommend the books for schools. It was expected that the committee members should go carefully through the books. There was a set of 3 books. Two of the three books were sent to the committee members for review. The third book was not complete and therefore only the cover (without content) was sent along with the first two completed books. Rest of the committee members rated the last book—third book (only cover without content) better than the first two books. It was such a bad situation. He brought it to the notice of concerned. He carefully scrutinized. Some of the books and found some of those books were lousy! They inculcate wrong notions in the mind of young students. In one book temperatures of some stars was given say red-4000, yellow-5000, green-7000, blue 10000, violet etc. As there are no green or violet stars, he expected that their temperatures should have not mentioned. In the same book mathematical calculations were expected by mixing say 4 red stars, 2 yellow stars and some other stars and getting the total temperature on which further calculations were to be done. He expected that absurd combinations could have been avoided by giving relevant examples in practice or reality. There was one book entitled 'Energy makes it go'. He questioned why the little of the book is not—'Energy makes it stop'. His intention was we should not nourish the biased view about any concept. Energy can be many things and title should be more general.

There is one interesting instance about his appointment at Chicago in Fermi's place. They offered him tremendous amount of money, three or four times of what he was getting as a salary! It was staggering! The letter continued with above offer as 'we had very much like to have you'. Feynman reflected back that offer in following words—'After reading the salary, I have decided that I must refuse. I would bother about a wonderful mistress.. her spending this huge amount, property or wrongly... . All this bother would make me uncomfortable and unhappy. I wouldn't be able to do physics well, and it would be a big mess! I can't accept the offer!'

Feynman was really a wonderful man unfathomable in his capacities and abilities, mischievous, still so much human in nature. He was more like a friend worthy to be in maximum contact. This jubilant source of inspiration for scientists and especially for physicists was extinguished in 1988. It was indeed a great lost, making us uncomfortable and unhappy.

19

S. Chandrasekhar

S Chandrasekhar has become a legendary figure for his outstanding contributions to astrophysics, physics and applied mathematics. He was the lonely wanderer in the byways of science. He tried to unravel unknown areas of science and through them in main stream however he remained detached from that area as soon as he got satisfied with whatever he wanted to do in that area. He fully experienced the loneliness of intellectual life. He was the person of enormously high standards, determined, idealistic, brilliant, modest, genial, self effacing, rigid, convincing and patient. He had effortless ease in handling mathematics. He used to live in nice presentable form—well dressed, elegant and with good tastes. He accepted the life as it came to him; the only aspiration for him was to develop science. His conviction was that work was the only panacea on any problem especially for loneliness and grief. He was meticulous worker and theorist. He was not interested to carry experimental work but used to utilize the observations extensively. By his patient and unassuming but definite approach he got the recognition, through quite late as the dazzling star

amongst the scientist. As he has said earlier “the moral is that a certain modesty of approach towards science always pays in the end” It came true in his case. His critics did not have the modesty to say. I am going to learn from what physics teaches to me... they wanted to dictate how physics should be. He was open-minded and had no jealousy about anybody. He was a person with high virtues.

S. Chandrashekhar was born on 19th October 1910 at Lahore (now in Pakistan). His father was C.S. Ayyar. He was deputy accountant general of Madras State. His grand father was Ramananathan Chandrasekhar. He was educator and administrator. In his meagre salary also he maintained home library. It was big family with 5 sons and 3 daughters. It belonged to *Shaivite Brahmans*. The family was progressive and educated. Sir C.V. Raman, noted Indian Nobel laureate (1930) was Chandrasekhar’s uncle. Sitalakshmi was Chandra’s mother. She managed big family and progressed. As a child Chandra was healthy, handsome, clever and mischievous. During his early days his father influenced him and carefully brought him up. His mother nourished with love and affection. She was his motivating force. Ramanujan, C.V. Raman, Saha, Ghosh, Mukharjee were the people who deeply impressed his young and creative mind. He made up his mind to pursue pure science just from his high school days. He was little more matured from his early days. He avoided confrontations right from the beginning. His mother wanted him to be great, greater than his uncle C.V. Raman. It had deep roots in his mind. He felt very sorry when his mother expired when he was abroad. He missed her badly on all occasions of his crucial importance of his life. His father wrote him numerous and illustrative letters and shaped his life. S. Chandrasekhar was also in full rapport with his father through letters. His father informed the death of his mother and wrote ‘Bear Patiently’. He took this lesson throughout his life. There were many occasions where son and father differed. Both of them showed mutual understanding and respect about each others views but Chandra followed his own course. His father wanted him to do ICS, wanted him to take a job in India and so on. Chandra remained strictly vegetarian throughout except he could eat eggs at his father’s advice. His father wrote him once ‘Live in Rome as Romans do’. He remained vegetarian as a matter of habit and not on religious grounds.

In fact he was atheist. According to him there was ample room for atheism in the Hindu religion. When Chandra was elected to Trinity Fellowship he sent the telegram to his father—"Elected to trinity fellowship stop wish mother alive stop. Please no paper publicity" This shows his feelings about mother and modesty. On other occasion when Raman offered him post his father reacted "My advice, keep off his orbit" This advice was given by his father because he was knowing Chandra's capabilities. He did not want to have greatness because of relationship with C.V. Raman. Self-respect was important for both of them. In short his mother, father and Ramanujan were three personalities in his making. There was good family background, conducive for education. He could get in contact with many great people.

One more personality to be noted is his wife—Lalitha. They knew each other since 1930 and were in correspondence. When Chandra saw her after six years he reacted 'she was more than a dream... quite real'. Lalitha's father Doraiswamy was a medical officer in Indian Army. Lalitha also had progressive, educated background especially due to her aunt sister Subhalakshmi. She had good career in physics. They were more than a match for each other. They got married on 11th September, 1936 in Tirupathy temple at Tiruchanur near Madras. It was the simple marriage. Lalitha played pivoted and important role in Chandra's life. Chandra reacted "she has been the motivating source and strength of my life. Her support has been my mainstay during times of stress and discouragement. She has shared my life selfless, devoted and ever patient and waiting" Chandra's wife was the only person who had deeper association with him next to his scientific pursuits.

Chandrasekhar completed his education from Presidency College, Madras. He got M.A. in 1930. He left Bombay for Trinity College, Cambridge by steamer Lloyd Triestino on Government of India Scholarship. There were some serious problems even for his admission to Trinity College. Finally he succeeded. He completed his Ph. D. in 1933. He was elected the fellow of Trinity College. This honour earlier was only given to Ramanujan. He joined Yerkes Observatory, Williams Bay, Wisconsin as assistant professor by the end of 1936 and rose to

Morton D. Hull distinguished service professor in 1952. Then he shouldered the responsibility of the Astrophysical Journal at Chicago from 1952 to 1971. Then he remained in the University of Chicago. He got the voluntary retirement in 1980 and he was privileged to be Professor Emeritus up to 1983. He however remained at Chicago working quietly till his death on 21st August 1995.

He was much impressed by the company of F. Milne, Dirac and Sir Arthur Eddington at Cambridge. He was in contact with many great scientists and had cordial relationship with them. The list is exhaustive but to name the few will suffice- N. Bohr, Fowler, Raman, Bhabha, Bragg, E. Fermi, Fyson, Millikan, Rutherford, Planck etc. He widely travelled over many countries lecturing, participating in symposia and seminars. If anybody asks to note Chandra's weaknesses or flaws with any of his acquantee the unanimous answer that would come is—NONE. Such was this great man of science.

Chandrasekhar was thinking about White Dwarfs right from his departure for England in 1930. He studied the problem in greater depth in during following years meticulously and as per his nature, He put his work in the meetings of Royal Astronomical Society, London. These meetings used to be held on every second Friday of the month. These meetings were the academic high points. Renowned persons used to attend them and if the paper was accepted with full debate on it issue, it was sigh of (recognition) by the scientific world. It was the meeting of 11th January 1935 when Chandrasekhar read his epoch making work about White Dwarf. He was sure to get it accepted but to his surprise it was highly criticized and in fact ridiculed by the authority like Sir Arthur Eddington. It was devastating experience and Chandra was distraught. Eddington reacted "your mathematics may be right but your physics is wrong". It was more surprising that Eddington was knowing that work and they even met the earlier day. No criticism was offered and it was publicly that he denounced. His style and prestige was such that nobody can openly defend Chandra's work and cross Eddington. During following years people used to support Chandra. Fowler's reaction is worth noting—they are being superstitious...and what havoc it makes in science! Other remark was—'Eddington's arguments tended to shift with time' Eddington continued criticising and it was still more surprising. Once, after Chandra's paper read on Friday he reacted on next day—"Our beliefs on Saturday must be different from Friday." Anyway Folwer, Dirac and Bohr along with many other scientists were on the side of Chandra and Milne was on Eddington's side. In a due course of time 'Chandra' got the justice but what a humiliation he had to face! One must admire that with such an experience at the earlier stage of life he contributed such a great deal to science. He had 51 PhD's at his credit. He had written 9 monumental and excellent books on various subjects. His selected papers are turned into 6 Volumes. He used to publish 7 to 8 papers every year for about 50 years. These papers were of high calibre and with new openings. It can be said about him that he was great scientist as good scientists add to human knowledge, the great ones open new doors. More important is the remained without malice to anybody even to Arthur Eddington.

If Chandra's work would have been accepted earlier, scientific developments would have accelerated very fast. His work 'Chandrasekhar Limit' is as follows. Energy is produced in the interior of stars by fusion reaction. As this energy comes out it exerts a pressure called the radiation pressure. It is balanced by the gravitational force pressing all the mass of the star towards its centre. Consider a large star that has run out of fuel and can't produce sufficient energy any more. There is no balance between radiation pressure and gravitational force. As a result star shrinks and shrinking star heats up and it can no longer hold its material in the form of molecules. They break up into electrons and nuclei called 'Degenerated matter'. This principle stops the star from shrinking further. The degeneracy now balances the gravitational force and we have a White Dwarf. Chandrasekhar found out the limit for the mass of star collapsing to White Dwarf as 1.445 to the mass of sun, the stars with mass less than this limit can only be converted to White Dwarfs and the stars with higher mass than this limit will have different fate. The principal of degeneracy can't save it from collapsing. This work was labelled 'basically wrong research'. In fact it has roots to 'Black Holes' and many other important discoveries that were delayed.

Chandrasekhar has developed how own style of research. 'Research Chandra style' it had three components teaching, research and writing. He used to work in unknown area for 5 to 8 years non-stop with full devotion and for 12 to more hours a day all days of the week. Then write a nice, flawless, treaties, leave that area and again enter into new area was his way, He had constant rejuvenation of himself by entering new fields. Thus he wrote the following books:

1. An Introduction to the Study of Steller Structure (1939)
2. Principals of Steller Dynamics (1943)
3. Stochastic Problems in Physics and Astronomy (1943)
4. Radioactive Transfer (1950)
5. Hydrodynamic and Hydro Magnetic Stability (1961)
6. Ellipsoidal Figures of Equilibrium (1968)
7. The Mathematical Theory of Black Holes (1983)
8. Eddington: The Most Distinguished Astrophysicist of his time (1983); and
9. Truth and Beauty: Aesthetics and Motivations in Science (1987).

Many of these books were translated in Russian and few in Japanese. These books were reprinted. He personally liked his book 'Radioactive Transfer'.

Chandrasekhar was given many honours, medals and prizes in reorganisation of his outstanding work. They include—Fellow of Royal Society of London (1944), Adams Prize (Cambridge University) (1947), Bruce Medal (Astronomical Society of the Pacific) (1952), Gold Medal (Royal Astronomical Society) (1953), Member of the National Academy of Sciences (1955), Rumford Medal (American Academy of Arts and Science) (1957) Royal Medal (Royal Society of London) (1962), Shrinivasa Ramanujan Medal (Indian National Science Academy) (1962) National Medal of Science (United States) (1966), Padma Vibhushan Medal (India) (1968), Henry Draper Medal (National Academy of Sciences) (1971), Smoluchowski Medal (Polish Physical Society) (1973), Dannie Heineman Prize

(American Physics Society)(1974) Nobel Prize for Physics (Royal Swedish Academy shared with W. Fowler)(1983), Dr. Tomalla Prize (RTH, Zurich)(1984) R.D. Birla Memorial Award (Indian Physics Association)(1984) and Vainu Bappu Memorial Award (Indian National Science Academy) (1985) Total 18.

Apart from his science, he had a deep interest in literature and music. His grand father's library imbibed in him the craze for reading which lasted for ever. His likings include Dostoevski, Chekhov and Tolstoy (Russian); Virginia Woolf, T.S. Eliot, Thomas Hardy, John Galsworthy, Bernard Shaw, William Shakespeare and Ibsen (English). In his writings-letter, books and conversations, it used to be reflected. He was extremely a good teacher. In his lectures one can feel electricity, music and rhythm. He believed learning means teaching, it is inseparable pair. He used to drive twice a week 100 miles to teach two of his students Lee and Yang. These two students got Nobel Prize in 1957. His whole class was the recipient of the prize thus. He was the fast driver and used to drive between Yerkes Observatory at Williams Bay, Wisconsin and University of Chicago. He had a strong belief in the potential of young generation. He used to mix with them with vigour and wit. He also liked children especially the children of his colleagues. When he visited Russia first he had impression of about it as that of young man with full of ideas...indomitable moral courage... indefatigable physical strength. He was given very warm and unforgettable welcome at various places.

He was on journey from Odessa to Istanbul across the Black Sea. In his cabin there were three ladies 2 Russians and 1 German. They were not happy to have him amongst them. The arrangement was made that they should go to bed and then he be entered in cabin. He entered and concluded that port hole be closed and he wished according to which they did not respond. Water rushed inside and he reacted 'the only time I have ever taken shower with three ladies' He faced such type of racial discrimination number of times but he took it sportingly.

One lady at dinner after receiving Nobel Prize asked him "The work you are recognised for was apparently done fifty years ago. What have you been doing since?" Chandra responded "They also serve who only stand and wait"

The lady reacted "Oh! You have been waiting for the Nobel Prize all these years?" Chandra kept silence assuming that lady was not knowing the poetry of John Milton.

He was a nice entertainer at the group discussion. He used to tell the stories of great scientists and alike. Once he gave the lecture and there were three black boards. He wrote nicely on all boards and concluded his lecture. One participant interrogated... 'Paragraph 8 line 11 seems to be wrong' Chandra remained calm without turning to his statement. When he was asked about his calmness he responded 'It was not a question, it was a statement, and it is mistaken' reflecting his utmost confidence.

He used to tell his students the story of *Arjuna*(Best amongst the five *pandavas*—without referring the names) aiming at the eye of the bird. He was seeing only eye and nothing else. This used to illustrate concentration and he had every right to preach it.

Another story he used to tell was that of stumbling stone. Many suffered out of that stone but nobody tried to turn it aside. The person who tried to turn aside got golden treasure below it. His approach in searching by ways of science was similar to turn aside the stumbling stone.

He started his career in the astrophysics journal in 1952 with remarks—'He is a theoretical. He does not understand astronomy'. He brought high status to the journal with greater income, greater circulation, greater volume in pages and all with increasing surplus. He was the autocrat of the editor's desk, He was firm and rigid about his convictions, He remained more in tune with Cambridge England rather than Cambridge Massachusetts USA. When he left the journal in 1971, he responded 'the journal has left no residue of feeling in me'. Such was his great accomplishments.

He was tried to join some place in India but without success. Dr. S. Radhakrishnan, Indira Gandhi, Dr Bhabha Nehru, Sarabhai, his father, C.V. Raman etc tried to persuade him for the purpose. He remained in America for the sake of better pursuit of science—laboratory, library, people and students—

better environment for study and interaction. He even did not think of leaving Chicago.

His work will have long lasting impact on the frontiers of science in the fields of Dynamical Friction, Relativity, Black Holes, Big Bang Theory, White Dwarfs, Stability of very fast moving objects, Properties of matter in the Magnetic Field and alike. He was nicely blended person with philosophy and science, hardship and discipline; curiosity and patience, gentleness and culture. He was the rarest Indian born scientist with such extra ordinary capabilities and qualities. Every Indian should be proud of him.

20

Tom Kilburn

'Computers' was the most important invention since fire or perhaps wheels. They have practically entered into every field like banking, industries, research, communication, defence, environment, medicines and what not! We are living in a 'Computer Age'. Personal computers have become household word. The speed with which computer have encompassed our lives is amazing. In order to illustrate impact of television Canadian philosopher Marshall McLuhan said—'The world had become a global village". We have no words to express the impact of computers. We are 'Spell Bound'. It is worth to know about computers and it is absolutely necessary. The hows and the history of most machinery are intimately connected. The first computer is ABACUS as old as 5000 years. It is derived from Greek word abax—meaning calculating table covered with dust. In 1942, Blaise Pascal derived mathematical machine to help his father's business. It used decimal system and used 0 to 9 numbers. It had eight wheels and quite huge. It was non-portable computer.

Because of it high calculating ability it was an important step. Now Pascal is honoured with one of the high level computer language is named after him (PASCAL). In 1694 German Scientist Leibniz tried to build machine which can add, subtract, multiply, divide and extract square root. He also introduced 'reckoning' or 'stepping' while solving mathematical problem. It is breaking a problem in step (logical) The machine however did not work. Leibniz is the pioneer in using binary system in computers 0 and 1.

Decimal system has many columns to express numbers. For example first four columns are Thousands, Hundreds, Tens, Ones.

Thus number 4237 has four thousand two hundred thirty seven. Contrary to this binary system will have first four columns as Eight, Fours, Two, Ones.

Therefore Number 8 is represented in binary system as 1000 (It has l eight 0 four 0 two 0 one). Number 7 can be (0111) extending some 5th column will be 16, 6th column will be of 32 and so on. Number 27 in binary system will be (11011) etc. Binary system has important role in electronics and computers. It has added 'astonishing speed element' in computation without mistake. As there are only two alternate 0 or 1, yes or no etc.

In 1812 Charles Babbage had made an attempt to provide results of mathematical problems by means of mechanical machine. He had invented a 'Difference Engine' which could carry out a sequence of mathematical operation—one at a time. He is regarded as the 'Father of Computer's'. He further discovered in 1935 'Analytical Engine'. In 1890 Census machine was framed. In 1911 Hollerith joined Computing Tabulating Recording Company now known as IBM. He had contributed to some extent. Then in 1939 Mark I—partly electrical and partly mechanical adding machine came in line. It was quite big 15' long and 8'. Then there was important break through in February 1946 ENIAC (Electronic Numerical Integrator and Calculator). It was world's first general purpose digital computer. It was designed by John Eckert and Juan Mauchly at Moore School of Engineering of Pennsylvania. ENIAC occupied 3000 cubic ft area and had 18000 valves. It consumed large energy—140 KW power. The computer was programmed manually by setting switches and plugging unplugging cables. Further in the mid 1940's John Von Neumann is credited with the stored programme concept. In it the programme is represented in a form of suitable codes and stored in the memory. The programme can be read by computer function; the programme can be set or altered by changing or modifying it.

ENIAC did not possess the crucial attribute of stored programme control. The World's first successful stored programme computer was developed in a Bridgeford street building opposite Manchester University by Prof. Fred Williams and Prof. Tom Kilburn, aided by engineer Geoff Toothill on loan from telecommunications research establishment (TRE). The computer which filled the room was made from war time valves, cathode ray tubes, and wire and tin. It ran its first programme on June 21, 1948. Its memory capacity was only 32 words, it stored 2048 digits but it started a technological revolution. Until this breakthrough, computers had been just calculating machines. Though this, world entered the domain of real computers from the domain of calculators. The first programme was written by Tom Kilburn. It was a programme to find the highest proper factor of 2^{18} this was to be done by trying in single routine every integer from (2^{18} -1) = 262144-1 down word, the necessary divisions were done not by long division but by repeated subtraction of the divisor (because the Mark I only had a hardware substractor). About 1,30,000 numbers were tested, this involved 3.5 million operations (It could be 3.8 million operations, as Prof. Kilburn now recollects). The numbers tried were from 262143 (2^{18} -1) to 131072 (2^{17}). The correct answer was obtained in 52 minutes run. There were just 7 instructions. Information was displayed in 'reverse binary' system (e.g. 6 number would be displayed as 0110000...00 and not 00...000110) These results appeared in September issue of magazine Nature 162 Volume pages 487 (1948). Tom Kilburn's reaction on June 21, 1948's achievements was as—"...the most exciting time was June 1948 when the first machine worked without question. Nothing could ever compare with that".

William's reaction was—'A programme was laboriously inserted and the start switch was pressed, immediately the spots on the display tube entered the mad dance. In early trials it was a dance of death leading to no useful result and what was even worse, without yielding any clue as to what was wrong. But one day it stopped and there, shining brightly in the expected place was the expected answer. It was a moment to remember. This was in June 1948 and nothing was ever the same again.'

There was time race going on in converting 'stored programme Computer concept' into reality at four places namely:

1. University of Pennsylvania EDSAC (1949) was the result,
2. John Van Neumann at Princeton University on the Institute of Advanced study machine (IAS),
3. Maurice Wilkes of Cambridge University, and
4. University of Manchester.

Early memory technologies involve:

1. Vacuum tube based flip flops. It is expensive and a bit of information is given in each flip flop.
2. Acoustic delay lines. In this digital information was stored as a 'sound' waves in a meter length tube of mercury. The waves propagated down the length of the tube where at the far end they were converted to electronic signals, amplified and feedback in other end. Information was periodically available. It was used in EDSAC (1949), DINA (1949), UNIVAC (1950) and EDVAC (1951) computers.
3. Cathode Ray Tube (CRT) like the monitors used as a display device in today's computers. It involved scanning electron beam to deposit a charge on the surface of a phosphor coated screen. Binary information 0's and 1's could be stored in a different sized charges on the phosphor screen. It was truly 'Random—the time to access any bit was constant'. Memory contents could be directly read by observing the pattern of glowing dots on the phosphor screen leaked away after a fraction of a second. It is therefore

necessary to refresh CRT memory continuously. Eventually ways were found to efficiently refresh the screen. This improved method was subsequently used in Manchester Mark I (1949), IAS (1952) Princeton and IBM's 701(1953) Computers.

CRT memory design was first successfully used in BABY (1948) computer. It is also referred as The Manchester Automatic Digital Machine (MADM). Mark I prototype or better as Small Scale Experimental Machine (SSEM). It marked the history of computer. CRT memory design was called Williams Tube, better would be to call it William S. Kilburn Tube. In a process by December 1st, 1947, 2048 bits were being stored on a standard single 6" diameter CRT introducing 'dot-dash' and 'focus-defocus' methods of operation of the CRT and the design of hypothetical computer was made. Williams arranged to read the change and then rewrite it continuously at electronic speeds so that information could be kept permanently, this process was called 'regeneration' and the principle is still used today to replenish charge on modern integrated circuits RAMS (Random Access Memory) Williams was a genius electrical engineer and remained so all along. He looked to this profession as worthy and said 'why is it laudable and proper to show that a thing can be done but quite improper to do it?' He was working with Telecommunications Research Establishment (TRE) and was secondly by Tom Kilburn, He designed the CRT for memory storage and Kilburn used it effectively in BABY for the first time.

Professor Sir Frederic Colland Williams FRS (1911-77) was always known to his friends and collaborators as Freddie Williams, or more often just 'F.C.'. He was born at Romiley, close to stock Port. He was educated at Stockport Grammar School and University of Manchester in the department of engineering and gained B.Sc. (1932) and M.Sc. (1933) degrees. He was awarded Ferranti Scholarship by IEE to do two years research at Oxford University. He was awarded DPhil (1936) for work on circuit and valve noise. He then took up the post of Assistant Lecturer in his old Department of Manchester. He carried research in Electronics and published some 20 papers. In 1939 he left the university after getting Doctor of Science (D. Sc.) and joined Telecommunication Research Establishment (TRE).

TRE then moves to Malvern in 1942. During the war years he made out standing contributions to the electronics of radar and other military equipments—one was 'Operational Amplifier'. He made major contribution to the development of IFF (Identification of Friend or Foe) systems for aircrafts and to AI (Airborne Interception) systems which provided on board equipment allowing aircraft to automatically track and intercept other air craft. Another system to which he contributed was Oboe (a precision ground controlled blind bombing system). At Malvern he was renowned for emphasis on 'circuit designability'—the development of circuits whose operation can be predicted accurately before they are built. It was obviously crucial in the war years. A characteristic of his circuit designed was that it was generally voltage based rather than current based. He ran a small group in a room in the cricket pavilion of Malvern College. He had a reputation as prolific generator of ideas. He also liked to give flamboyant names to it's devices like 'Phantastron' He developed CRT storage system (1946-47) known as Williams Tube. In 1945 and 1946 he visited the Radiation Laboratory at Massachusetts Institute of Technology (MIT) in USA. In 1946 he also visited the Moore School of Engineering, home to EMAC where research on CRT was also underway. After coming back he concentrated on CRT storage By November 1946 he could demonstrate the use of CRT to store binary digit. F. Williams was appointed to the chair of Electro-technics at the University of Manchester in December 1946. He was seconded by Tom Kilburn since 1942. Their group was known as 'Think Tank' and problem solver for radar. He also designed magnetic drum for storage. He filed patents about his research in order to save foreign currency as other should not derive the benefit of his research and go ahead. He then concentrated on Electrical Engineering problems fully for 25 years (1952-77). He unravelled many problems related to circuits and motors. He was always supportive and helpful to others. He received numerous honours in his life – most notably FRS (1950), Faraday Medal (1972) and Knight Bachelor (1976).

Tom Kilburn was born on August 11, 1921 at Dewsbury, Yorkshire – England. He was educated at Cambridge University where he read mathematics. He got his BA and MA degrees from that university. He got his Ph. D. (1948) for cathode ray storage and D. Sc (1953) from Manchester University. On his call up after graduation in 1942 he was order to take a City and Guilds crash course in electricity, magnetism and electronics in London and then to report to the Telecommunications Research Establishment (TRE) at Malvern. Kilburn reflected on his first meeting with new boss and later Collaborator F.C. Williams: "I didn't know Freddie Williams until that day and in effect he said oh God, you don't know anything? And I said 'no'. That was the sort of relationship at the start. But of course by the time we left Malvern—that was four years later—the relationship was quite different".

Tom Kilburn quickly made an impression with his keen mind and supreme engineering ability in the design of electronic circuitry and made many contributions to the electronics of radar. He moved in 1946 to Manchester with Williams. By March 1947 Tom Kilburn had suggested an improved of sorting bits and by the end of 1947 they were able to store 2048 bits on CRT, having explored various techniques. Tom Kilburn submitted a report to the TRE management. This report—A storage system for use with Binary Digital computing machines (Progress report issued 1st December 1947) was circulated widely and influential in several American and Russian Organizations adopting Manchester developed CRT storage system. In early 1947 he attended series of lectures at National Physical Laboratory (NPL) given by Alan Turing. Turing had completed the design of NPL's computer based on mercury Acoustic Delay Lines as the storage device and the lectures were about that details. Kilburn was influenced by there lectures but in directly; and he resolved *not* to build a computing machine *like that* but to design and build CRT storage computer.

Tom Kilburn built Small Scale Experimental Machine (SSEM) 'The Baby' This tested in practice the ability of Williams tube and for the first time in the world of computer was built that could hold any small user programme in electronic storage and process it at electronic speeds. He wrote the first programme for it which first worked on June 21, 1948.

With successful results of 'The Baby'; the expanded team of Williams moved on to design and build a more powerful and usable computer—the Manchester Mark I (1949). In the autumn of 1948 the government had commissioned Ferranti

Ltd. to build a commercial machine to Prof. Williams's specifications as Ferranti Mark I (1951). Williams having many other duties, Tom Kilburn was senior full time worked on the project. Williams did not want to be diverted from a life in Electrical Engineering. Next machine that was developed was MEG, it was version of Mark I with floating point arithmetic added. Computing speed was issued by factor of 30. MEG first ran in 1954. Kilburn then explored the capability of transistors in computers with a magnetic drum store. Small version first ran in November 1953 and expanded version in April 1955. Ferranti Ltd. turned MEG into 'Mercury' with ferrite core store for RAM. 19 Machines were sold, the first in 1957. Alongside the continuous evolution of computer technology taking place under Tom Kilburn designed for large machine with transistors and magnetic core store and faster. It was called MUSE (for microsecond) and aimed for 1 million instructions per second. The project went slow and MUSE was rechristened Atlas (1962). Only three full versions of Atlas were built. Tom Kilburn's next project was to set up a new department. He was made a professor of Computer Engineering in 1960 and in 1964 the computer group evolved into the new Department of Computer Science. Tom Kilburn became head. Dai Edwards in charge of hardware and Tony Brooker in charge of software. In 1966 Kilburn and his team started work on their next machine MU5(1974). Tom Kilburn retired in 1981 handing over to Prof. Edwards the flourishing department with around 30 staff and annual in take of 100 students.

Tom Kilburn received large number of honours and awards over the years. For example : Fellow of Royal Society (1965), Emeritus professor, Eckert—Mauchly Award for Computer Architecture (1983) Royal Medal of the Royal Society (1978), Computer Pioneer Award, IEEE Computer Society (1982) etc. He is still quite simple and keeps away from all functions and publicity. He is widower. He prefers to be aloof. He is the pioneer of modern computer with memory storage. 21st June 1948—Monday was the historical day of his achievements. Manchester University is celebrating Golden Jubilee of his achievements with various International programmes. Kilburn has witnessed the change of the world due to extensive use of computers. He is extremely happy to look at it independently. It is surprising that Prof. Kilburn himself does not have even small personal computer. He is stunned with these developments. Tom Kilburn was only 26-year-old when 'THE BABY' worked. He was quite moderate economically (can be said as poor). He used to travel by train during those days and used to think and play with new ideas that he wanted to implement. His wife and son were with his father at Dewsbury. His baby computer was huge; it was 18 feet long and 8 feet high. It was getting hot when switched on and one was suspecting that it might explode. The people, who assigned, however, were sure that it wouldn't! He is proud of his achievements but he is more modest. He is sure that if Williams and himself would not have invented this storage mechanism some one else would have done it. He is so plane and straight forward. He feels that during coming fifty years there will be revolutionary changes in the field of artificial intelligence. He also is confident that science can not achieve more or even equal intelligence as that of human brain. It is difficult to imagine so and its consequences.. He is the person who believes in the work only without considering the benefits, honours and prizes resulting out of that. He is happy contented man without malice for anybody. Let long happy and contented life be at his store!

He had said in 1992 as "...the fundamental difference between a theoretician and engineer is that an engineer is away and doing something once he has grasped that there is a way of doing something and theoretician is strangely enough most of the time lagging behind, cleaning up that's the best word I can use..."Kilburn himself is a nice example of an engineer defined by him but an exception himself to his theoretician's definition.

Let us review the present state of affair in computer field broadly after knowing Kilburn's work. The first generation of computers used vacuum tubes, second generation used transistors, the third generation used integrated circuits (ICs) and the fourth generation used Very Large Scale Integration (VLSI) of millions of components on single silicon chip. This increased speed, reliability and efficiency many fold. At the same time reduced cost, size, and ease of handling to lower and lower level. Personal computer is now household appliance. They consist Monitor (Output), CPU (Central Processing Unit), keyboard (Input). The central processing unit itself has three units, namely Arithmetic and logical unit (ALU), control unit (CU) and memory unit. Basic necessary components in computer are:

1. System Unit
2. Monitor
3. Key board
4. Floppy disk drive
5. Hard disk drive.

Optimal components include Mouse, Printer, Scanner and light pen. Computer has two main types of memories :

A. Internal/Primary/Secondary Memory

(*i*) RAM—Random Access Memory. It is temporary. It is lost when power is cut. It is volatile memory—read write memory. User can also change the data feed in this memory.

(*ii*) ROM—Read Only Memory. It is permanent. Non-volatile memory. Information is written onto the chip during manufacturing. Information can only be read and no new information can be written on ROM.

B. External Memory

Floppy disc or hard disc. It is magnetic memory. Capacity of hard disc is very high compared to floppy disc.

Output can be in the form of monitor; printer – three types (character printer, line printer and laser printer) and plotter.

It is ever changing field. One must be quite alert and efficient while working in the field. 'Survival of the fittest' is the rule in this field. Prof. Tom Kilburn, however will survive for ever (be eternal) in this field because of his epoch making contribution!

21

Stephen Hawking

Stephen Hawking is one of the very few scientists who became legend in their own life time. He is most famous living scientists. He is remarkable 'mute genius in wheel chair'. He is scientist as well as remarkable person. He is a sensitive, humorous, ambitious and occasionally wilful human being. His life is fascinating and therefore our taste for wonder is well catered for. He is a multidimensional man and mass media have exploited his aspects to the greatest extent. He is referred as Einstein's heir, second Einstein, commander/master of universe or physicist who could analyze the mind of God, His work regarding Black Holes and origin and nature of universe is outstanding. At the very early age of 21 he had to suffer by chronic disease called—motor neuron disease (as called in England or Amyotrophic Lateral Sclerosis (ALS) in America). It is a disease of nervous system in which control on muscles is lost. He is in the state of paralysis, speechless and unable to

lift his head. He has to depend on all activities on a nurse, a student or a colleague. Still in his eyes one can see that divine twinkle of genius and his face is quite likely. His life and work is astonishing. It is a challenge to medical science. More interesting feature of his life is, though he is suffering from such a disease he is able to work with a speed, dimensions and with miraculous results. Shakespeare says "Sweet are the uses of adversity". It is perfectly true in Hawking's case.

It is an amazing coincidence that Stephen Hawking is born on 8th January 1942 which is the three hundredth anniversary of the death of one of history's greatest intellectual figures, the Italian scientist Galileo Galilei. Moreover since his undergraduate days Hawking has been a keen follower of the philosopher Karl Popper. The main trust of Popper's philosophy of science is that the traditional approach to the subject 'the scientific method' as originally espoused by Galileo is in fact in adequate. In scientific method steps involved include observation/experiments, general theory to explain, propose hypothesis based on general theory, further experimentation to verify hypothesis which will prove or disprove and repeat. Popper stands his process on its head and suggests following approach. Take a problem. Propose a solution or a theory to explain what is happening. Work out what testable propositions you can deduce from your theory. Carry out tests or experiments on these deductions in order not to prove them, but to refute them. The refutations combined with the original theory will yield a better one. These two approaches are in fact quite opposite to each other but can led to better and valid answer to the problem. Hawking works very much on intuition. Science as it develops today is by both these approaches.

Hawking's mother was Isobel. She was a daughter of the doctor from Glasgow. Her father taught her with many difficulties across. She graduated from Oxford and when she was serving as the secretary at medical research institute, she came in contact with Frank Hawking—Stephen's father. Frank was born in farmer's family. He also took his medical education in quite adverse situation. He was recognized as an expert on the diseases caused in tropical area. Frank and Isobel were learned and had good collection of books. They wanted Stephen to learn in a good school like 'Westminster school'. He could not appear for scholarship examination of the said school, and as fees were too high, he could not be admitted in that school. He was then admitted in St. Albans School. He was eccentric and awkward, skinny and puny. He used to jabber always and he could not talk clearly. He was figure of class room fun, teased and occasionally bullied, secretly respected by some but avoided by most. St. Albans School was the perfect environment for cultivating natural talent. He came across finally—an excellent teacher in that school. Mother also shaped his life. He was bad in sports but good in cycling, cross country, running, war games, drills and parades. He had deep interest in Extrasensory Perception (ESP) earlier but then left. He used to visit chemical plants, power stations and museums. He developed aptitude for mathematics when he was 14. In 1958 along his friend, they built computer called LUCE—the Logical Uni selector Computing Engine. It was of little use however, due to bad and loose soldering.

At the age of 17 with many difficult examinations he got in Oxford University college. In a tutorial class he was the only student to complete one difficult problem with elaborate proof. He was further ahead of many text books. He was very quick in solving the problems as compared to his classmates. He could complete 3 years course with 1st class and got B.A. (Hons). He then joined Cambridge in October 1962. Oxford is first University in England and its university college is established in 1249. Cambridge was started in thirteenth century. Trinity is its renowned college. Oxford is a spread city. That university is referred as 'A University in a City' whereas Cambridge is called 'A City in University'. Cambridge is always dominated by academia'. He was placed with Dennis Sciama and not with Fred Hoyle. After one year of Ph. D. course his health problem started. There was speech impediment. Fortunately on the new year day he got to know Miss Jane Wilde in a party. This turned his life. He was at the time in depression, drinking and listening the music with high volume. He was confused and lacking the will to live. He was remembering a boy who died of leukaemia next bed and thought that his condition was much better and due to his marriage with Jane Wilde, he tried to live with lot of activity and engagements. They got three children. The marriage took place in July 1965 in the chapel of Trinity

Hall. First son Robert was born in 1967, daughter Lucy was born in 1970, and the third son Timothy was born in 1979. Jane could do Ph. D in Spanish language. It was a nice couple with lot of understanding and respect about each other. Jane was raised as Christian and she has a faith in God. Hawking does not believe in any faith or God. In his opinion pure mathematical reasoning can be override any need for God. Anyway science may one day answer the question 'how?' but not 'why?'

Stephen's nature is 'fighting' and has an aptitude for dispute, he loves nothing more than good argument. Along with his research, his contribution as a writer and social worked—woman students, plight of poor, environment and disarmament (are some of his areas of contribution). He also to maintain good relations with his first wife Jane and departed in 1990. He got married in September 1995 with Elaine Mason—his nurse and devoted companion for last seven years. Elaine Mason is the former wife of the man—computer engineer—David Mason. David gave to Stephen chair mounted computer. The tiny movements of his fingers, lips and muscles (very weak) are converted into words on computer screen. Walt Woltosz from California gave him the programme called Equalizer. He could therefore communicate better. Stephen and Jane were enthusiastic hosts and use to celebrate many family programmes. This is to illustrate wary nature and eccentricity of Stephen.

Cosmology is the study of universe. It is the biggest of big sciences in terms of idea, mind and mathematics. Pencil and paper are its equipments. Einstein put forth general theory of relativity. It is also called general theory of gravity. It says that due to gravitational forces of steller bodies' space time continuum gets curved. Einstein gave some equations in this connection and are called equations of universe. Planets move around the sun in elliptical orbits with the exception of mercury. Mercury when comes nearer to sun it changes its path. This can be explained by Einstein's Theory. This theory demolished the difference between straight and curved lines. Gravitation was discovered by Newton first and then the branch of mathematics 'Calculus' was discovered by him in order to explain it. It is probably only case in which physics has taken a lead over mathematics.

As per Einstein's special theory of relativity one can not decide the absolute speed of the object, it is always relative. He also proposed four dimensions to explain the universe—length, breadth, thickness and time. It is based on two facts:

1. Laws of nature are common to all observers; and
2. Velocity of light is constant.

This theory resulted into 4 revolutionary points;

1. Mass of the object depends on its speed;
2. Mass and energy are inter convertible $E = mc^2$;
3. Object in motion contracts in the direction of motion; and
4. Time is relative.

There are four basic forces acting in the Universe :

1. Gravitational
2. Electromagnetic
3. Strong, and
4. Weak

Sub atomic particles like proton, neutron and electron have dual nature i.e. particle + wave. They can be referred as 'wavicles'. Einstein up to the beginning of 1920 shared the Newtonian idea of a static universe. But within ten years, observations made by Edwin Hubble with a new and powerful telescope on a mountain top in California had shown that the universe is expanding. The universe was not static but evolving. Einstein later described his attempt to hold the universe still as 'the greatest blunder of my life'. If galaxies are getting apart in expanding universe, that means that long ago they must have been closer together. The idea that the Universe was born in a super dense, super hot fire ball known as Big Bang is now a cornerstone of science. This theory took over fifty years to become developed. During the period quantum theory which transforms our understanding of the very small also developed. The discovery of

Pulsars in 1967 is the direct proof of big bang theory or expanding universe. Pulsars are self revolving Neutron stars and emit radio waves after particular fixed gap of time. Neuron stars are resulted from supernova explosions. Stephen Hawking tried to combine quantum theory and general theory of relativity to explain universe and atom. Quantum theory considers sub atomic particles and their movements and actions. These particles have both state and speed combined. They are not independent properties. Radiations are not emitted continuously but in term of quanta (groups, units). It was proposed by Max Planck of Germany in 1900.

Big bang theory is supported by following proofs:

1. George Gamow as long back as 1948 expected left over (background) radiations from big bang. Around 1965 these radiations are detected as microwaves. By 1976 theory was established and Steven Weinberg was able to write best selling book—'The first three minutes'. He also got Nobel Prize.

2. The known mass in space consists of 75% hydrogen and 25% Helium

3. Satellite 'Cosmic Background Explorer' was sent in space in 1989 and its records are in favour by 1992.

4. This Big Bang created matter, space, energy and time.

Back hole is another concept that was rooted around 1960. Astronomers knew that stars with three times matter as that is sun would end up with 'A Black Hole'. American relativist John Wheeler dubbed/named them 'Black Holes' in 1969. 'Collapser' is the better word to understand Black Hole—'Anything ın the vicinity falls in but nothing could emerge'. Cosmic egg highest density—singularity theory is the origin of universe some 15 billion years back. Cosmic egg can be looked upon as super dense Black Hole. Roger Penrose one of the greatest authorities in mathematics and Geometry of Birck back college in London worked on Singularity Theory. Hawking also worked with him. Hawking could elaborately study Black Holes. His conclusions are the basic matter for researches in the field like—

1. Tiny Black Holes emit radiation but under certain conditions they could explode. Radiations emitted are known as Hawking Radiations.

2. Black Holes have event horizon and nearby pair of particles is produced one goes in black hole and other is emitted out. His paper 'Particle creation by Black Holes' was published in 1974. Black Hole is some region in space that exerts powerful gravity which act like gigantic vacuum cleaner and crushes to infinite density and vanish forever. It slows down time and stretch the space. Not even light can escape.

Origin of universe is still a mystery. It is open ended puzzle. Various models are emerging:

1. No Boundary Model of Universe.

2. Universe is Self Contained.

3. Universe is Simple and can be explained in Two Simple Terms—'Contraction and Expansion'.

4. Present Universe is at the verge of Big Crunch and Continuous Expansion.

5. Stephen Hawking is the Man to lead the way to formulate a Grand United theory or a Theory of Everything.

6. String theory—Super String Theory etc.

In all these points Stephen Hawking has contributed some or great extent.

One of the phenomenal contributions made by Stephen Hawking in popularising astrology to all the people of the world is the book 'A Brief History of Time'. He wrote this book with view to get appropriate reward in terms of money to support his family. Mitton was the person who fully cooperated with Hawking. Mitton was administrative head of the Institute—Institute of Astronomy on the outskirts of Cambridge. Earlier it was headed by Fred Hoyle and Donald Lyndan- Bell. Hawking worked at this place three mornings a week.

Milton describes him as a human magnet in the world of Physics. Hawking was never interested in observational astronomy but in Theoretical Physics. His approach was to use head, pen/pencil, paper and computer and quite rarely telescope. Milton recalls Hawking as irritable and impatient. He was over demanding from colleagues in terms of work loads. He always wanted things done yesterday because he works at such an intense pace putting great demand on himself. Penrose has pointed however unusual cheerfulness and sense of humour in the face of adversity with Hawking.

'A Brief History of Time' was published by Bantam Books of USA. The person who was instrumental in this publication was Peter Guzzardi. Hawking was offered 2.5 lakh dollars as an advance of royalty for US and Canada. Writing of the book was completed by August 1985. It was published in 1988 and got wild applause all over the world. The first 40,000 print run was in the market and Bantam realized two of the pictures were at wrong place and wanted the books back to be corrected. When they enquired with the book sellers about this they surprised to know that all books were already sold. Such was the craze for the book. Within 4 months 5 lakh copies of the book were sold in America and more than 10 million copies are sold world wide. The book was leaving the book shelves faster than the printer could produce new copies. The mystery of book's success is by any measure as baffling as the mystery of origin of Universe. Hawking's mother Isobel has commented...the reasons are comple...the book is well written, pleasurable to read...the ideas are difficult, not the language. He does not talk down to his readers.. He believes that his ideas are accessible to any interested person.. it is controversial but it stirs through. "Certainly his fight against illness has contributed to the book's popularity but he did not collect his academic and other distinctions (including Book's success)' because of Motor Neuron Disease. There is one interesting event that should be quoted about book's cosmopolitan appeal. Russian physicist Andrei Linde, was flying across America soon after the publication of the book. Next to him was seating a businessman who was reading Hawking's book. Their conversation started:

"What do you think of it" Linde asked.

'Fascinating' said the business man. 'I can't put it down' 'Oh that is interesting' the scientist replied. 'I found it quite heavy going in places and didn't fully understand some parts'.

At which businessman lean towards Linde and said 'Let me explain' The book is translated in 22 languages.

An ex- ABC news producer—Gordon Freeman was able to see the potential of Hawking's book as a film. He did not however wanted to make a straight documentary of Hawking's life and work. There were too many of its kind. He met Steven Spielberg (Producer of Jurassic Park) at Los Angles in this connection. Spielberg's involvement brought the scheme into high profile and got the finance. When Spielberg and Hawking met at Hollywood the focus of attention was Hawking and not demigod Spielberg—was quite a feat. The film was produced with three million dollar budget by Hickman, Freedman and Morris. Hawking was enthusiastic and patient during filming. He used to joke. Morris noticed Hawking's fascination with Marlin Monroe on which he reacted 'I suppose you could say she is the model of the universe'. The film was completed by 1991.

There were so many honours and awards given to Stephen Hawking. Some of them are given here to illustrate his absolute 'greatness' :

1. 1974 Fellow of Royal Society. It was just at very young age of 32
2. 1975-76 Six Awards :
   (*a*) Eddington Medal from the Royal Astronomical Society in London
   (*b*) Pius XI medal from Vatican
   (*c*) Hopkins Prize
   (*d*) Danni Heinemann Prize from USA
   (*e*) Maxwell Prize
   (*f*) Hughes Medal of Royal Society

3. 1979
   (*a*) Lucasian Professor at Cambridge the honour (Newton got 310 years back).
   (*b*) Honorary fellow of University College where he studied for under graduate course.
   (*c*) Man of the year by the Royal Association for Disability and Rehabilitation.
4. 1980 Commander of British Empire (CBE) by Elizabeth—II
5. 1982 Four honorary doctorates of universities i. Leicester, Britain ii. New York and iii. Princeton—USA iv. Notre Dam Paris.
6. 1989 Israeli Wolf Foundation Prize along with Penrose.
7. Cambridge University gave him honorary doctorate. It is an exceptional thing that person is getting honorary degree from the university in which he is working.
8. 1989 Companion of Honour by Elizabeth—II.

He wrote many research papers and two other books named 'A Short History' and 'My Experience with ALS' He was the co editor of the book 'General Relativity...An Einstein Centenary Survey (1979)' To his bad luck he had to operated for Tracheostomy in 1985 in which he lost his voice. Fortunately his life was saved by doctors as they were aware of his case and health problems. It happened in Geneva at the European centre/ observation for nuclear research (CERN) Hawking had more time in the Department of Applied Mathematics and Theoretical Physics (DAMTP) DAMTP has the atmosphere of free communication that is much needed for creative and innovative work. Many great people were also around to interact and discuss. Stephen remained there irrespective of many offers of better choice. Hawking was also able to work with America theoretician Kip Thorne for one year on a scholarship at Caltech—

California Institute of Technology. Caltech is the west coast's 'centre of excellence or global village' for science and technology.

Above account clearly supports that 'The sky is no limit in the career of Stephen Hawking'. Many article in prestigious magazines appeared like "The Universe and Dr. Hawking" New York Times Magazine, 23 January 1983 by Michael Harwood. The book written by John Boslough—'Beyond the Black Hole, Stephen Hawking's Universe' London, Fontann 1985 is also elaborate. Many TV broadcasts, his personal interviews and experiences by great people of science and media, his visits to many countries and renowned people leave no doubt but he is a 'cult' person, fascinating, alive like electric wire and he will emerge with still new ideas with his most active brain and unending demand for more work by himself and others. Let the world witness many miracles out of this giant of science and hope he will also miraculously have quite longer life.

Index